THE

REAL

A STUDY THROUGH THE BOOK OF REVELATION

JESUS

The Real Jesus
© Church of St. John the Divine, Houston TX
All rights reserved.
Published in Houston, Texas by Bible Study Media, Inc.

Paperback: 978-1-942243-58-8
E-Book: 978-1-942243-59-5
Library of Congress: 2022902979

Printed in the United States of America.

TABLE OF CONTENTS

Introduction

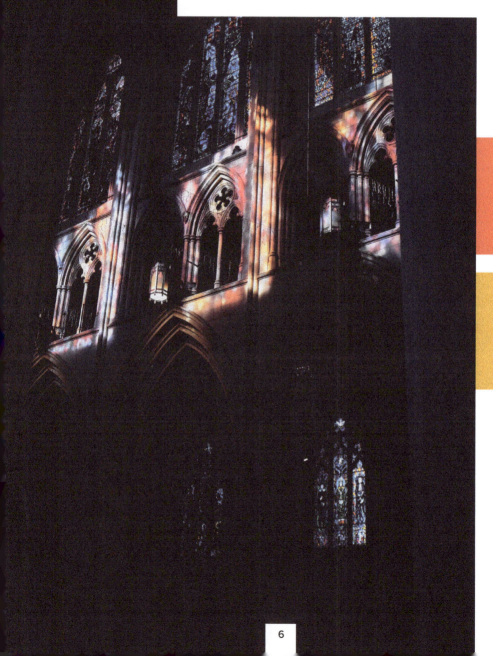

WELCOME

Have you ever wondered what the future holds for this world? Is this world spinning out of control? Where is God when the going gets tough? What does eternity look like? Jesus said that in this world, we will have trouble. But we can take heart—Jesus has overcome the world (John 16:33).

The book of Revelation was written to give us hope. Our heavenly Father desires that his children live with peace in their hearts, no matter what is going on in the world around them. This book reveals the power, majesty, and authority of Jesus Christ. Our world may seem out of control, but Jesus is sovereign. Our trials may feel hopeless, but Jesus holds us secure.

We often think of Jesus as the gentle Shepherd, the Suffering Servant, or the coming King. Revelation reveals the truth of Jesus in all his power and glory. And Revelation also uses the image of Jesus as the slain Lamb. In the natural world, a slain lamb is defenseless. To the modern world, a slain lamb is powerless—and the biblical image an oxymoron. How could a slain lamb be powerful? Revelation will help us see that the deep meaning of the slain lamb is the cross. Sometimes we are tempted to soften the truth of the cross and its impact on the world. But this study will reveal the true, eternal power of Jesus's work on the cross.

This last book of the Bible is different than studying other books. As you read the daily devotionals and participate in small groups, pray that God will help you glean the most out of The Real Jesus. The book of Revelation is full of metaphors that can be confusing, but this study guide provides additional information and application that will clarify the meaning for you.

Finally, Revelation 1:3 states, *"Blessed is the one who reads aloud the words of this prophecy, and blessed are those who hear, and who keep what is written in it, for the time is near."* Do you want to be blessed? Then step out in faith to study this majestic book, filled with the power and glory of Jesus Christ.

- MEG RICE

INTRODUCTION

Imagine you are John, an apostle of Jesus Christ. You are the only one of the twelve disciples still alive—all the others have died for their faith. Meanwhile, you have been exiled to the island of Patmos to silence you from proclaiming Jesus as the long-awaited Messiah, the Redeemer. Suddenly, during your prayer time, you are given an amazing vision and revelation directly from God and told to write it down.

Once again, the ministry of Jesus overwhelms you, informs you, and brings you back to who you are—the one whom Jesus loves. As the last living apostle, you are entrusted with this powerful message for the church today and the church to come.

Revelation can be divided into three parts:

"*What you have seen,*" the vision and words that we read in chapter 1.

"*What is now,*" the letters in chapters 2 and 3 to the seven churches of Revelation.

"*What will take place later,*" from chapter 4 to the end of Revelation. This is God's explanation of the end of this age, how and why it will occur.

In this final book of the Bible, God uses symbolism to communicate his prophetic message to the world. The Old Testament used similar symbolism, which at times can be confusing. Throughout history, Christians have established several schools of thought about interpreting this book.

Most Christian interpretations fall into one or more of the following categories:

- **Historicism**, which sees Revelation as a broad view of history.

- **Preterism**, in which Revelation primarily refers to the events of the apostolic era (first century) or, at the latest, the fall of the Roman Empire;

- **Amillennialism**, which rejects a literal interpretation of the millennium and treats the content of the book as symbolic;

- **Postmillennialism**, which also rejects a literal interpretation of the millennium and sees the world becoming better and better, with the entire world eventually becoming "Christianized;"

- **Premillennialism,** which is based on a literal interpretation of Revelation 20 and believes that Jesus will return to earth before the millennium, for a thousand years;

- **Futurism**, which believes that Revelation describes future events (modern believers in this interpretation are often called millennialists); and

- **Idealism or Allegoricalism**, which holds that Revelation does not refer to actual people or events but is an allegory of the spiritual path and the ongoing struggle between good and evil.

No matter what interpretation you adhere to, God is sovereign, and his Word is true. There will be a time when *"the earth will be filled with the knowledge of the glory the Lord as the waters cover the sea"* (Habakkuk 2:14).

The veil between the reality of earth and heaven is thin. As you study Revelation, you will see that what happens in heaven has a direct correlation to what happens on earth. Evil exists and is powerful, but the slain Lamb Jesus is more powerful, and he will defeat Satan and his forces. Satan's tactics have not changed since the Garden of Eden. He is a manipulator, a liar, and a deceiver. But God encourages believers with this vision and the words of Scripture. Jesus said in John 8:31, *"If you abide in my word, you are truly my disciples, and you will know the truth, and the truth will set you free."* The only way to identify the lies of Satan is to know the truth of God's Word.

Over the next few weeks, you will get a glimpse of the judgment of God, the sovereignty of God, the power of God, and the mercy of God. You will see that all of history has been moving towards the culmination of this age and the birthing of a new age, the eternal age. As with childbirth, the delivery begins slowly but progresses with ever-increasing suffering and pain until a new birth occurs.

Keep your eyes on Jesus, in all his glory, walking among the churches. He is ever-present, all-knowing, and all-powerful to guide, strengthen, and direct his people. In his hands are the seven stars, which are the angels of the churches. Jesus directs the angelic messengers of God to supernaturally support those who follow Him. These churches are representative of churches throughout the ages, and the letters to the churches apply to us today.

As you progress through this study, know that eternal victory is assured. Jesus will be victorious. His followers will be ushered into a new world, a new age where mankind will finally be in the presence of God, and all will be glorious.

"'Behold, the dwelling place of God is with man. He will dwell with them, and they will be his people, and God himself will be with them as their God. He will wipe away every tear from their eyes, and death shall be no more, neither shall there be mourning, nor crying, nor pain anymore, for the former things have passed away.' And he who was seated on the throne said, 'Behold, I am making all things new'" (Revelation 21:3–5).

This is the promise of Revelation.

DAILY DEVOTIONALS

Each week introduces a section of the Book of Revelation to teach key facets about God and our relationship with him. The Daily Devotions navigate through the book verse by verse, one chapter at a time, helping you delve deeper into the Scriptures and discover biblical connections. The Small Group study guide explores major themes in the Book of Revelation. Each set of weekly devotions is ordered and designed to be read alongside of the Study Guide sessions. The devotions serve as a foundation and complement to support the key points and themes explored in the Study Guide group sessions.

How to Begin

1. Set aside time to spend with the Lord each day.
2. Pray and ask the Lord to reveal himself to you through the pages of his Word.
3. Read and reflect on the appointed Scripture reading and devotion for each day.
4. Use the notes space to record insights that strike a chord, as well as journal ideas or questions that are new or relevant.
5. Review the Study Guide session once weekly. You may also want to view the video ahead of the group session.

As you do these things, the Lord will surely bless you with the riches of his Word.

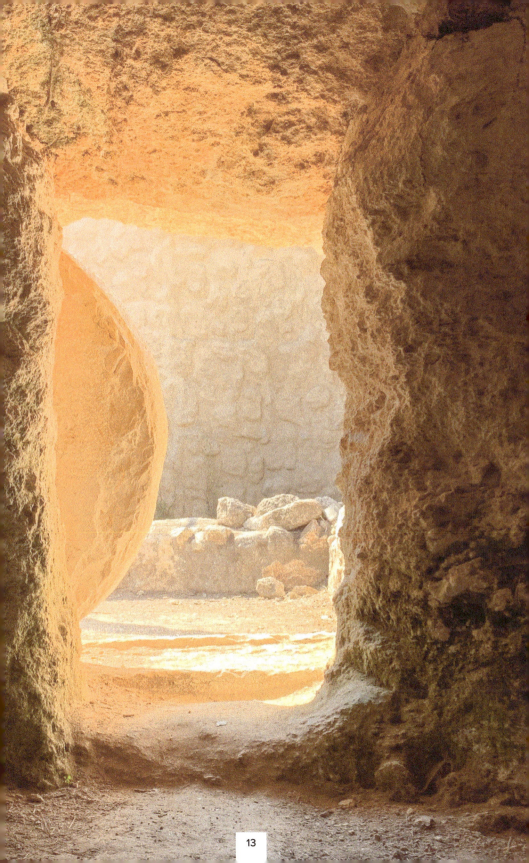

WEEK

1

THE LIVING SAVIOR AND HIS CALL TO THE CHURCH

DAY 1

JESUS IN GLORY

REVELATION 1:1–8

"Achoo!"

A nearby voice says, "Bless you."

We all want to be blessed. Living life under a blessing is a good thing. The first three verses of Revelation promise that those who read and take to heart the words of Revelation are *blessed*. How can this be, when this final book of the Bible is filled with weird, supernatural revelations? Revelation has been called a book that's hard to understand but difficult to forget. Let's find out why.

The final book of the Bible speaks of things to come, but more importantly, it is the revealing or unveiling of Jesus Christ. Revelation explains why Jesus had to be crucified to save man from the clutches of sin and evil. It also reveals the power of Jesus that will put all things right by his coming in glory.

> "The revelation of Jesus Christ, which God gave him to show his servants what must soon take place. He made it known by sending his angel to his servant John, who bore witness to the word of God and to the testimony of Jesus Christ, even to all that he saw. Blessed is the one who reads aloud the words of this prophecy, and blessed are those who hear, and who keep what is written in it, for the time is near." (1:1–3)

The words *"made it known"* come from the Greek word σημαίνω, or sémainó, to give a sign. Revelation is full of symbols or signs that reveal a greater truth. These same symbols are used in other parts of the Bible. This rich imagery is all a part of the revealing of Jesus.

The book of Revelation is unique in that God dictated it. Its words carry the voice of God about himself and his Son, Jesus. That is why the person who hears and takes to heart the words of this book is blessed.

The apostle John is the scribe of this book. The recipients are the seven churches of the Revelation. These churches were in existence at the time of the writing of Revelation but can represent churches throughout the ages.

"Grace and peace to you from him who is and who was and who is to come, and from the seven spirits who are before his throne, and from Jesus Christ the faithful witness, the firstborn of the dead, and the ruler of kings on earth. To him who loves us and has freed us from our sins by his blood and made us a kingdom, priests to his God and Father, to him be glory and dominion for ever and ever. Amen. Behold, he is coming with the clouds, and every eye will see him, even those who pierced him, and all the tribes of the earth will wail on account of him. Even so. Amen.

'I am the Alpha and the Omega,' says the Lord God, 'who is and who was and who is to come, the Almighty'" (1:4b–8).

The above verses are a beautiful description of the Holy Trinity, the mysterious unity of the Father, Son, and Holy Spirit.

Jesus is alive and well. He isn't sitting in heaven, basking in glory. He is moving and active in our world and in our personal lives. Notice that love is the impetus that compelled Jesus to die on the cross and transform us into kingdom-builders and priests who represent Jesus on earth.

Do you ever feel like you don't belong to this earth? That you were made for something better than this world? You were! We were created to be citizens of a heavenly kingdom. Abraham felt this way, too (Hebrews 11:10).

When Jesus came to earth the first time, it was to save the world through the cross. He promised that he would return. When speaking about his return or second coming, Jesus says:

"For as the lightning comes from the east and shines as far as the west, so will be the coming of the Son of Man [Jesus's favorite name for himself]" (Matthew 24:27, 30).

Why does the world mourn? Possibly the Jews mourn because they did not believe Jesus was their Messiah when he first came to earth. The rest of the world mourns because of our waywardness and sins that put Jesus on the cross. As we see the glory of Jesus Christ displayed in Revelation, we will see clearly that we are not worthy of him or his sacrifice.

The point of this introduction is that Jesus will return. It is a promise.

A friend of mine was questioning me about the second coming. She had lost her mother and asked a question I would like to share with you: "If we die before the global return of Jesus, then does the second coming of Jesus happen for that person at the time of death?" This comment reminded me of John 14:1–3, where Jesus promises to come back for us.

Does death scare you? Are you concerned about a loved one that has died? If we have faith in Jesus, our death marks a passing from one reality to another. We are no longer in this world; we are in the perfect kingdom that we were created for: the kingdom of God—and we have Jesus himself as our escort!

> "Jesus said to him, 'I am the way, and the truth, and the life. No one comes to the Father except through me" (John 14:6).

JESUS IS HERE TODAY

REVELATION 1:9–20

Have you ever had a vision that seemed so real that you could remember vivid details? John the disciple did, and his vision is recorded in Revelation. It was a vison so clear and with such amazing detail because God *"made it known"* directly to John (1:1).

John was told to write down the vision and send it to the seven churches—real, first-century churches in Asia Minor (modern-day Turkey). Jesus is coming in his glory to continue his teachings to his beloved churches.

> "Then I turned to see the voice that was speaking to me. And on turning I saw seven golden lampstands, and among the lampstands one like a son of man, clothed with a long robe and with a golden sash around his chest. The hairs of his head were white, like wool, like snow. His eyes were like a flame of fire, his feet were like burnished bronze, refined in a furnace, and his voice was like the roar of many waters. In his right hand he held seven stars, from his mouth came a sharp two-edged sword, and his face was like the sun shining in full strength" (1:12–16).

John wants us to know the circumstances of this letter. He was on the island of Patmos as a prisoner because of his faith in Jesus. He was *"in the Spirit on the Lord's day,"* which means he was worshiping (1:10). Suddenly, BAM—a voice as loud as a trumpet commanded him to write. The first coming of Jesus was incognito; not many noticed the baby in the stable. The second coming will be a full-blown light show, complete with sound effects.

When you read these verses, what do you sense? Remember, Revelation is full of symbols we have seen in Old Testament prophecies and other Scripture. Here are a few symbols in this passage that reveal or unveil realities about Jesus.

1. His <u>clothing</u> is like the ancient priestly garments—a long robe and a golden sash, symbolizing Jesus as the High Priest who intercedes to God for the people (Exodus 28:39; 39:29; Daniel 10:5; Hebrews 4:14).

2. His <u>white hair</u> denotes the timelessness and purity of his wisdom (Daniel 7:9).

3. His <u>eyes, like blazing fire,</u> reveal his judgment. Nothing is hidden from the eyes of him to whom you must give account (Daniel 10:6; Hebrews 4:13).

4. <u>Bronze</u> is symbolic of the bronze altar in Exodus, where the ancient Israelites slaughtered the sacrifices for the people's sins. His bronze feet speak of the fact that Jesus himself went through the fires of judgment on earth and came forth as pure (Exodus 27:1–8; Ezekiel 1:7; Daniel 10:6).

5. His <u>voice, like rushing water,</u> is powerful and majestic, like a storm at the beach (Psalm 29:3–4; Ezekiel 43:2).

6. The <u>sharp, two-edged sword</u> coming out of his mouth is symbolic of the penetrating power of the Word of God, which is called the sword of the Spirit (Ephesians 6:17; Hebrews 4:12).

7. His <u>face, shining like the sun</u> must have taken John back to the mountaintop experience when Jesus was transfigured before his eyes (Matthew 17:2). There, John saw only a token of the glory of Jesus; now he is seeing it full throttle.

No longer is Jesus the Suffering Servant; now he is the victorious Living One in the fullness of his majesty and power.

> "When I saw him, I fell at his feet as though dead. But he laid his right hand on me, saying, "Fear not, I am the first and the last, and the living one. I died, and behold I am alive forevermore, and I have the keys of Death and Hades" (1:17–18).

John's reaction is a human response to experiencing the glory of the Lord Christ. We can't take it. But Jesus gently touches his beloved John and reassures him. Jesus is claiming what God claims; that he is the First and Last, the Alpha and Omega. Jesus never claimed to be anything less than deity. Jesus also claimed his humanity. He died on the cross, but death could not hold him. He holds the keys to death and Hades (1:18). In Scripture, keys represent authority. Jesus has the authority over his own death, which extends to his authority over our physical death. Hades represents the abode of Satan, the enemy of our spiritual lives. Jesus has control over that, too!

> "Write therefore the things that you have seen, those that are and those that are to take place after this. As for the mystery of the seven stars that you saw in my right hand, and the seven golden lampstands, the seven stars are the angels of the seven churches, and the seven lampstands are the seven churches" (1:19–20).

Jesus is in the fullness of his power and glory, and look what his concerns are—his churches. The seven angels were assigned to each church to guide and minister as Jesus directs. Even today, Jesus is present among his churches, as near as the person in the next pew (Matthew 18:20).

Revelation is divided into sections that the Scripture gives us. John writes *what he has seen?* which is chapter 1 of this vision. Then in chapters 2–3, he writes *what is now?* the instructions and warnings to the existing seven churches. Finally, John writes *what will take place later?* from chapter 4 through the end of Revelation.

I love that God does not want us to be in the dark. He wants us to be at peace. When things get bad, Jesus has everything under control. Does that give you assurance when your life seems out of whack? It should.

> "You keep him in perfect peace whose mind is stayed on you, because he trusts in you. Trust in the LORD forever, for the LORD GOD is an everlasting rock...for behold, the LORD is coming out from his place to punish the inhabitants of the earth for their iniquity" (Isaiah 26:4–5, 21).

....

....

....

....

....

....

....

....

....

....

LOVE COMES FIRST

REVELATION 2:1–7

On a trip several years ago, I went to Ephesus. It is a remarkable archeological restoration. You can walk down the marble boulevards and stand before the magnificent library. But it's all in ruins. What happened? It was destroyed by the Goths in AD 262 and rocked by an earthquake in the sixth century. Silt built up in the river that led to the ocean, damaging the harbor and interrupting trade. Additional earthquakes and governmental changes contributed to the decline of this once-proud city.

As we begin our study of the seven churches, we will see a common format in each one.

1. Introduction: First, the angel tells who sent the letter. Each one is from Jesus, and he describes himself with a specific characteristic to communicate his message.

2. Positive deeds: Jesus praises the church for their good works.

3. Negative deeds: Jesus points out ways that the church is falling short.

4. Promise of rewards: The reward belongs to the overcomers—to those who take the criticism to heart and persevere in faith for what God has called them to be.

This chapter is like a report card for the churches. And as we study their grades, we need to put the microscope on our own faith to see if we have the same issues that need addressing as the churches. We also need to take stock of our local church. Are we falling into any of these categories? What would Jesus say to our church? What areas need improvement?

Some theologians believe that each of these churches represents a particular season of church history. If so, Ephesus represents the time from about AD 70–160. After the death of most of the apostles and those with first-hand knowledge of Jesus, a second generation came along. The passion of the first generation was replaced with complacency and doctrinal compromise in the second generation.

First, Jesus describes himself to Ephesus:

> "To the angel of the church in Ephesus write: 'The words of him who holds the seven stars in his right hand, who walks among the seven golden lampstands" (2:1).

Jesus is the one in control. He is not distant; he is among them—he is in their midst and observing them. His control over the angel of that church is complete. The same is true for us. He is right there, communicating with us and guiding us through the Word and prayer (Psalm 23:3; Romans 8:14).

Second, Jesus commends them:

> "I know your works, your toil, and your patient endurance, and how you cannot bear with those who are evil, but have tested those who call themselves apostles and are not, and found them to be false. I know you are enduring patiently and bearing up for my name's sake, and you have not grown weary" (2:2–3).

So far, the Ephesians have an A+ record. So let's turn the microscope towards us. Am I working hard for God's kingdom? Do I persevere when the going gets tough? Do I test my beliefs to make sure that false doctrine is not seeping in? Do I endure hardships for God?

Third, Jesus tells them what is wrong.

> "But I have this against you, that you have abandoned the love you had at first. Remember therefore from where you have fallen; repent, and do the works you did at first. If you do not repent, I will come to you and remove your lampstand from its place" (2:4–5).

With all the good things that the Christians of Ephesus are doing (2:2–3), it would be easy for us to assume that all is great. But what is their motive? These verses reveal that their first love, the fervent love they showed as new believers, is no longer there. Perhaps they are "doing church" and not abiding with Jesus. This is a danger for us as well. As we grow in our faith, we can get distracted. Sometimes our worldly concerns pull us away, and sometimes our kingdom work pulls us away from time with the King. But Jesus wants our hearts more than our works (1 Samuel 15:22; Hosea 6:6).

If the Ephesians don't change, Jesus is clear, the lampstand of their church will be removed. Sadly, that is what happened. No longer is there a Christian presence in Ephesus.

But Jesus then commends them again:

> "Yet this you have: you hate the works of the Nicolaitans, which I also hate" (2:6).

Who were the Nicolaitans? They were Christians who had professed faith but practiced loose sexual morals. They claimed piety and special privileges from God, but their lives reflected evil. Do you know anyone like that? Are there ways that you profess faith but live like an unbeliever? The church is called to correct sin in faithfulness to God and love for one another (Matthew 18:15–20).

The punishment is severe, but look at the reward for those who respond to Jesus.

> "He who has an ear, let him hear what the Spirit says to the churches. To the one who conquers, I will grant to eat of the tree of life, which is in the paradise of God" (2:7).

The fourth part of the letter promises the right *"to eat of the tree of life."* This is the tree that we read about in Genesis 2:9, and it means that we have eternal life in paradise with God.

The lesson to the church of Ephesus warns us: If your love for Jesus is growing cold, remember how hot it was when you first came to faith. Repent, ask for forgiveness, return, and do what you did when you first came to faith. Take time with your beloved Jesus. Read the Word, journal your prayers, and sing to the Lord. The Holy Spirit will help your heart remember (John 14:26) and reignite your love for Christ.

....

....

....

....

PERSECUTION AND POWER

REVELATION 2:8–11

The second church is Smyrna, located in modern-day Izmir in Turkey. It represents church history from AD 160–320, the age of the martyrs. A succession of ten Roman emperors, from Nero to Diocletian, persecuted Christians in Smyrna with ever-increasing torment.

First, the introduction reveals a characteristic of Jesus:

> "And to the angel of the church in Smyrna write: 'The words of the first and the last, who died and come to life" (2:8).

Jesus assures these Christians that he is God and he has defeated death.

Next, he reflects on their positive deeds.

> I know your tribulation and your poverty (but you are rich) and the slander of those who say that they are Jews and are not, but are a synagogue of Satan. Do not fear what you are about to suffer. Behold, the devil is about to throw some of you into prison, that you may be tested, and for ten days you will have tribulation. Be faithful unto death, and I will give you the crown of life" (2:9–10).

I love the fact that Jesus says at the beginning, "*I know*." The Christians at Smyrna were very poor. Perhaps because they did not worship Caesar, they were denied jobs and buying power. During this time, the Christians were also robbed as a form of persecution. But because they were outcasts in society, they could not seek legal recourse. Amid their persecutions, Jesus assures these Christians that he sees what is going on. He knows.

Even in their poverty, Jesus calls them rich! They have what matters.

Usually, at this third point in the pattern of these letters, Jesus admonishes the church for her negative deeds. But notice the difference with the church at Smyrna: they are doing what the Lord has asked of them. There is not one thing that the Lord has against them.

Instead, Jesus prepares them for more persecution to come. Jesus tells them that Satan is behind all this evil coming against them. Their faith is being tested. Why do we need to be tested like that? God knows our hearts. But he allows testing to build our faith. Passing a test makes us stronger believers.

> "In this you rejoice, though now for a little while, if necessary, you have been grieved by various trials, so that the tested genuineness of your faith—more precious than gold that perishes though it is tested by fire—may be found to result in praise and glory and honor at the revelation of Jesus Christ" (1 Peter 1:6–7).

Jesus says that some of them may even die. History records the death of the pastor of Smyrna, Polycarp, who was martyred in AD 155.

The overcomer will not be hurt by the second death. The second death is the lake of fire, hell, but it will not affect them. They are protected and guarded by the one who beat death and came back to life. They will be victorious, too, through this Righteous One.

So what happened to this church that was under so much persecution? It is the only one of the seven churches that survived Roman and Muslim persecution. Today the churches of Smyrna are alive and active.

In each of the specific churches, Jesus closes with "*He who has an ear, let him hear what the Spirit says to the churches*" (2:11). Do we have an ear to hear? Are our hearts open to constructive criticism of our faith and our church? Remember, the Lord disciplines those whom he loves (Proverbs 3:12). He wants us to live in the hope of his calling (Ephesians 1:18). But first and foremost, he wants our passionate love and devotion. Without that, all else fails.

> "Abide in me, and I in you. As the branch cannot bear fruit by itself, unless it abides in the vine, neither can you, unless you abide in me" (John 15:4).

The Christians at Smyrna faced persecution and hardship because of their faith in Jesus. Are we willing to sacrifice for Jesus? Are we willing to go out of our comfort zone to help others? Will we be like the hands of Jesus to serve people around us (John 13:14–15)? Think about it your life. Who comes to mind? Pray for the faith to endure the testing that comes to all Christians.

Remember that your strength does not come from the greatness of *your* belief but the greatness of the *Person* in whom you believe.

....

....

....

....

....

....

....

....

....

....

....

....

....

....

....

....

....

....

....

....

THE STRUGGLE WITH COMPROMISE AND POWER

REVELATION 2:12–17

As we continue to hear what Jesus has to say to the churches of Revelation, we open our hearts to the Holy Spirit's conviction, to examine where we are falling away and where we need to return to our Lord.

Ancient Pergamum sat on top of a mountain overlooking the valley below. It was the capital of the Roman province and boasted a remarkable library. In fact, parchment was first used in Pergamum. It was also the center of pagan worship, where one of the first temples to Caesar was constructed. Pergamum also built a temple for healing, dedicated to the god Asclepius, whose symbol was a serpent. What does that remind you of? (See Genesis 3:1–6 with Numbers 21:9; John 3:14–15).

Pergamum is a sharp contrast to Smyrna. Where Smyrna endured outside persecution, Pergamum faced enticement and corruption from within. If the devil can't waylay people with persecution, he will entice and lure them into sin (2 Corinthians 11:13–14).

> "And to the angel of the church in Pergamum write: 'The words of him who has the sharp two-edged sword'" (2:12).

At the beginning of this letter, Jesus describes himself as the one who has the sharp double-edged sword. Hebrews 4:12–13 tells us that this sword can cut through our layers of disguise and deception and reveal our true motives.

We know that God disciplines those he loves (Proverbs 3:12), and he loves the Christians in Pergamum. When they are dirty from the world around them, he makes them clean. The sharp, double-edged sword cuts to reveal any infection of sin, so we can be made pure, holy, and healed.

The city of Pergamum is the most disturbing to me. It is described as the home of Satan, where he reigns. Yet even during such evil, the church is commended for faith amid persecution.

> "I know where you dwell, where Satan's throne is. Yet you hold fast my name, and you did not deny my faith, even in the days of Antipas my faithful witness, who was killed among you, where Satan dwells" (2:13).

Evil permeated this city, this throne of Satan. But those living surrounded by evil held firm to their Christian beliefs despite the pressures around them. These faithful Christians held on to the truth of Jesus, even in the face of

martyrdom as in Antipas. They proclaimed their faith at the risk of their own lives. These are the positive deeds that Jesus praises in their church.

But there are negatives.

> "But I have a few things against you: you have some there who hold the teaching of Balaam, who taught Balak to put a stumbling block before the sons of Israel, so that they might eat food sacrificed to idols and practice

sexual immorality. So also you have some who hold the teachings of the Nicolaitans. Therefore repent. If not, I will soon come to you soon and war against them with the sword of my mouth" (2:14–16).

In our culture, the "attitude of Balaam" can be seen in false teaching or false prophets. They may look the part of godliness, but they lead people astray. They compromise the commands and authority of God. Prosperity churches consume wealth like food sacrificed to idols. Liberal churches turn a blind eye to sexual immorality. Their attitude of "going along to get along" is one of Satan's best strategies—compromise from within (2 Peter 2:1).

The practices of the Nicolaitans represent unchecked ambition and power. Some think that they have a special relationship, an inside track with God. They believe that they possess superior knowledge about God and approach their flock with an air of superiority. Nicolaitans means "conqueror of people." They reveled in holding sway over other Christians. For them, ambition and power were their gods, but Jesus taught that humility is the path to greatness (James 4:6; 1 Peter 5:5).

How are we doing as a church, as individuals? Jesus declares that if the church doesn't expose false teachers, he will. The sword will peel away the darkness and reveal what is inside.

And for those who stand firm?

> "He who has an ear, let him hear what the Spirit says to the churches. To the one who conquers I will give some of the hidden manna, and I will give him a white stone, with a new name written on the stone that no one knows except the one who receives it" (2:17).

The promise of hidden manna represents the bread of life, Jesus. He will take these overcomers to a hidden place and feed them. He will give them a new name, a sign of intimacy and favor.

Pergamum represents church history from the rise of Constantine in AD 320 through the sixth century. It was a time of doctrinal debates within Christianity. Little by little, pagan practices replaced the pure faith and love of Jesus. Pergamum represents compromise with the world and turning from the commands of God.

> "I appeal to you therefore, brothers, by the mercies of God, to present your bodies as a living sacrifice, holy and pleasing to God, which is your spiritual act of worship. Do not be conformed to this world, but be transformed by the renewal of your mind, that by testing you may discern

what is the will of God, what is good and acceptable and perfect" (Romans 12:1–2).

Do our actions reflect our faith? Do we compromise our faith for the ways of the world?

Do we give a silent nod to pornography, the sex slave market that is so rampant in the world? Or do we do something about it, as God's people?

Do our lives reflect servanthood and not superiority with our brothers and sisters in the church? *"Clothe yourselves, all of you, with humility toward one another, for 'God opposes the proud but gives grace to the humble'"* (1 Peter 5:5).

....

....

....

....

....

....

....

....

....

....

....

....

....

....

....

....

....

WEEK

2

A SAVIOR WHO DOESN'T GIVE UP

DAY 6

A CALL TO PURITY

REVELATION 2:18–29

Today, we encounter the most corrupt of the seven churches—Thyatira. Despite their sin, Jesus has not rejected them. He is still walking among them and holding their star closely to himself while he warns them to repent. He is committed to helping his people walk victoriously through the temptations that come against them. He does that today for each of us. Sometimes we may think that we are too corrupt to belong to Jesus. But Jesus doesn't give up on us. He knows our sins, and he helps us escape our temptations (1 Corinthians 10:13).

Thyatira was thirty-five miles southeast of Pergamum. It was a relatively small city but had bustling commerce on a major trade route. Thyatira was known for its many trade unions, which gave special privileges to members but financial disaster for outsiders. Some theologians believe the patron god of Thyatira was a god of bronze.

> "And to the angel of the church in Thyatira write: 'The words of the Son of God, who has eyes like a flame of fire, and whose feet are like burnished bronze" (2:18).

Jesus introduces himself as the Son of God, making his deity and authority clear to them. His eyes are like blazing fire, which speaks of his ability to pierce through facades, pretense, and disguises. His feet, like burnished bronze, refer us back to the bronze altar of Exodus where the sacrifices were made for the sins of the people (Exodus 27:1–8). Jesus, the Son of God, can trample sin underfoot and severely punish wrongdoers.

> "I know your works, your love and faith and service and patient endurance, and that your latter works exceed the first" (2:19).

Again, Jesus sees and knows what's going on. Despite their circumstances, the people were faithful. But they needed correction; they needed to repent from their backsliding in what they were allowing.

> "But I have this against you, that you tolerate that woman Jezebel, who calls herself a prophetess and is teaching and seducing my servants to practice sexual immorality and to eat food sacrificed to idols. I gave her time to repent, but she refuses to repent of her sexual immorality. Behold, I will throw her onto a sickbed, and those who commit adultery with her I will throw into great tribulation, unless they repent of her works, and I will strike her children dead. And all the churches will know that I am he who searches mind and heart, and I will give to each of you according to your works" (2:20–23).

The story of Jezebel is recorded in 1 Kings 16 and 2 Kings 9. She was the daughter of the king of Sidon and married King Ahab of Israel. She hated righteousness and strived to obliterate God's people. This Jezebel in Revelation looks like she belongs to God, but she lives a life of immorality. Jezebel was one of the most evil women in the Old Testament. With her marital power, she promoted idolatry and the worship of Baal, the god of fertility. Baal's temples were filled with immoral sexual behavior, prostitutes, and orgies. Jezebel committed murder for a tract of land, and she tried to have Elijah killed. She was ruthless, a seducer of people. The spirit of Jezebel encompasses control and immoral behavior. This church in Thyatira allowed a false prophet and teacher to mislead the flock.

This time, Jesus doesn't tell the church to repent. He makes it clear that this woman and her cohorts have been given an opportunity to repent, and their path is set. Look at their future judgment:

1. Since Jezebel desires the bed so much, she will be condemned to a bed of suffering (2: 22).

2. Those who adopt her evil are given an opportunity to repent—but if they don't, they too will suffer intensely (2:2). This "whoredom" of spiritually playing around with other gods will result in pain and suffering. Sexually transmitted diseases, such as gonorrhea and syphilis, were common in the first century.

3. Children will be struck dead (2:23). This verse refers to spiritual death and does not necessarily mean children but those who are like Jezebel. Those she spawns will be spiritually dead and experience the second death of judgment.

4. *"And all the churches will know that I am he who searches mind and*

heart, and I will give to each of you according to your works" (2:23). These so-called Christians will not escape judgment. The result of judgment and discipline of the churches is a purified church.

5. The next warning is more vague but just as dangerous to those who "do not hold this teaching, who have not learned what some call the deep things of Satan" (2:24). What are Satan's so-called deep secrets? In the Bible, sexual immorality is linked with idolatry. To worship God and his Son Jesus is to be obedient to his teachings. But to fall into sexual sin involves desiring something over God, which is idolatry.

This may seem harsh. But remember, Jesus is still walking among this church in Thyatira. They are being deceived, and he wants them faithful. Today there are only a few ruins of Thyatira, in the modern city of Akhisar, in Turkey. There is no church in the city.

Historically, this church represents the time from the sixth century to the sixteenth century, during the Dark Ages, or the Early Middle Ages. The papacy in the church had huge political power. It was a hierarchal church that boasted reverence on the outside but was immoral and impure on the inside. Yet, during this time, monasteries also flourished and cared for the poor and sick.

For those who overcome this evil:

"The one who conquers and who keeps my works until the end, to him I will give authority over the nations, and he will rule them with a rod of iron, as when earthen pots are broken in pieces, even as I myself have received authority from my Father. And I will give him the morning star. He who has an ear, let him hear what the Spirit says to the churches" (2:26–29).

These overcomers will rule in the millennial kingdom with Jesus, and they will be uniquely equipped to rid the world of this controlling evil. The morning star is a reference to Jesus and the immortality that is assured to those who hold to the teachings of the Lord.

Thyatira's example shows us that we need to withstand the evil that seduces us into falling away from our Christian duty to be lights for Jesus Christ. Does our church leadership and teaching promote sexual purity? Does it offer a hand of welcome to all who come while teaching about the virtues of a life that reflects Jesus? Does our Christian walk exhibit sexual purity? The world's standards are not always the standards for those who follow Jesus Christ. He wants us to walk in freedom and holy love for one another.

"For you were called to freedom, brothers. Only do not use your freedom as an opportunity for the flesh, but through love serve one another" (Galatians 5:13).

STRUGGLE AGAINST SELF-SUFFICIENCY

REVELATION 3:1-6

In the letters to the churches, Jesus pleads from his heart. He pleads for Ephesus to go back to their first love, for Smyrna to hold firm amid persecution, for Pergamum to rid itself of false teachings, and for Thyatira to hang on to their righteousness and resist the spirit of Jezebel.

But for the church at Sardis, Jesus has nothing to commend.

> "And to the angel of the church in Sardis write: 'The words of him who has the seven spirits of God and the seven stars. I know your works. You have the reputation of being alive, but you are dead. Wake up, and strengthen what remains and is about to die, for I have not found your works complete in the sight of my God. Remember, then, what you received and heard. Keep it, and repent. If you will not wake up, I will come like a thief, and you will not know at what hour I will come against you'" (3:1–3).

Jesus describes himself as he did in chapter 1: He lives, he is in their midst, and he is in control. Sardis was situated on a mountain spur, where natural cliffs formed a steep and impenetrable wall. But the people of Sardis had a false sense of security, and the city was overrun. At times, we may think that we are not in danger to outside influences. Our eternal faith is secure in Christ, but our walk of faith can be paralyzed by sin and backsliding. The church of Sardis is a lesson to us.

The people of Sardis thought they were doing the work of God, but they were dead. This is a dangerous place to be. But Jesus was still among them, trying to draw them back. This church was extremely wealthy, and they had all they needed for a happy, joyous life. But they were dead.

Historically, this church represents the time from the last half of the sixteenth century, beginning with the Reformation, to the middle of the eighteenth century, continuing through the Second Great Awakening. After the Dark Ages, men like Martin Luther, John Calvin, and John Knox spread the truth that faith alone in Jesus Christ is sufficient to be saved and justified. Their preaching ignited a revolution in the church that was filled with the Holy Spirit. However, it was short-lived. The churches became tied to the states, and preachers were overworked. They were charged with huge areas of ministry to baptize, marry, and bury. This left them with little time for the study of God's Word. The life of the church started to die without careful study, preaching, and teaching of the Word.

So how did Jesus exhort the church at Sardis to reignite their faith? How do we reignite a faith that is in danger of dying out? Repent and believe.

> "Remember, then, what you received and heard. Keep it, and repent. If you will not wake up, I will come like a thief, and you will not know at what hour I will come against you" (3:3).

Repent of complacency, self-sufficiency, and self-advancement. At times overcoming our self-sufficiency can be the most difficult challenge. But we are saved by faith, not by works, so that no one can boast (Galatians 2:8–9). Cling to the grace offered through Jesus Christ. When we realize that all our works are like filthy rags (Isaiah 64:6), we are humbled and are ready to be justified by Christ's death on our behalf (Luke 18:9–14). We fall at the foot of the cross in submission and love.

> "Yet you have still a few names in Sardis, people who have not soiled their garments, and they will walk with me in white, for they are worthy. The one who conquers will be clothed thus in white garments, and I will never blot his name out of the book of life. I will confess his name before my Father and before his angels. He who has an ear, let him hear what the Spirit says to the churches" (3:4–6).

Those who overcome are promised a white robe of righteousness and purity before the Lord, eternal life with their name written in the book of life, and a special presentation at the throne of God. How do we overcome self-sufficiency and complacency? We fight against our flesh daily with time in God's Word, self-reflection, and prayer—asking the Holy Spirit to show us where the shadows of complacency are gaining ground.

We need to examine our motives as individuals and as a church. Are we seeking self-glory? Are we coming to the cross in our own power? Jesus settled all matters of our worthiness at the cross. When our life is laid bare before God, all our faults, failures, successes, and sins will be exposed. But for those who trust in him, Jesus will stand up and claim, "That one is mine." And we will be with him and enjoy him forever (Psalm 16:11; John 17:24).

....

....

....

....

....

....

....

....

....

....

....

....

....

....

....

....

....

....

....

....

....

....

THE GOLD STAR

REVELATION 3:7–13

The church at Philadelphia gets a gold star of approval from Jesus.

> "And to the angel of the church in Philadelphia write: 'The words of the holy one, the true one, who has the key of David, who opens and no one will shut, who shuts and no one opens. I know your works. Behold, I have set before you an open door, which no one is able to shut. I know that you have but little power, and yet you have kept my word and have not denied my name. Behold, I will make those of the synagogue of Satan who say that they are Jews and are not, but lie—behold, I will make them come and bow down before your feet, and they will learn that I have loved you. Because you have kept my word about patient endurance, I will keep you from the hour of trial that is coming on the whole world, to try those who dwell on the earth'" (3:7–10).

Jesus describes himself first as holy (3:7). He is the Holy One of God (John 6:69; Revelation 4:8), and he is true (John 14:6, Revelation 6:10)—qualifying him to have *"the key of David"* (3:7). The key represents authority. All Jews had a vision of the throne of King David to be everlasting. The Jewish leaders of Philadelphia must have thought that they were the rightful heirs of David's throne, but Jesus says that they are imposters and belong to Satan. Despite persecution from the *"synagogue of Satan"* (3:9), the Christians in Philadelphia have held firm.

The early Christian church not only suffered persecution from local pagans but also from the established Jewish leaders. But Jesus's words speak peace to the Christians of Philadelphia: *"I know your works....you have kept my word and have not denied my name"* (3:8). The church was suffering, and Jesus lets them know that he sees their faithfulness.

These Christians have the strength of the Holy Spirit within them, and Jesus says that this Spirit can be used to transform the world. They have studied the Word, they have not compromised or denied any aspect of Jesus, and they are ready for an open door to ministry. All they had to do was walk through this open door. The qualifications were in place. The church had little strength, but with the backing of Jesus, they had all they needed. Jesus encouraged Paul with similar words, "*My grace is sufficient for you, for my power is made perfect in weakness*" (2 Corinthians 12:9).

We sometimes wonder if we are ready for ministry. Are we equipped to accomplish the eternal works that are before us? This church in Philadelphia has "little strength," but they have not neglected to proclaim Jesus. They were steeped in the Word and followed God's Word. When he was on earth, Jesus encouraged his disciples, "*For truly, I say to you, if you have faith like a grain of mustard seed, you will say to this mountain, 'Move from here to there,' and it will move, and nothing will be impossible for you*" (Matthew 17:20). This little church exhibits that power does not come from the size of our faith but from the faithfulness of our Savior.

The church of Philadelphia will be rewarded and vindicated before those who are persecuting them. They will not experience "*the hour of trial that is coming on the whole world, to try those who dwell on the earth*" (3:10), the end of the age during a time called the tribulation. These Christians have already proven their faith.

Historically, this church represents the Great Evangelical Awakening in the eighteenth and nineteenth centuries. During that time, itinerant preachers traveled across America preaching the good news of Jesus. Missionaries from Europe and America crossed the oceans to India, Africa, Burma, and China. Millions were taught about the saving grace of Jesus and responded in faith.

> "I am coming soon. Hold fast what you have, so that no one may seize your crown. The one who conquers, I will make him a pillar in the temple of my God. Never shall he go out of it, and I will write on him the name of my God, and the name of the city of my God, the new Jerusalem, which comes down from my God out of heaven, and my own new name. He who has an ear, let him hear what the Spirit says to the churches" (3:11–13).

The church in Philadelphia has the greatest reward—a crown given to those who run the race well (3:7). These Philadelphians have already won the race. These Christians who have endured and held fast will be the pillars that every church needs as role models. They will be part of the heavenly Jerusalem, and their eternal home is secure. Finally, Jesus will write his name on them, "*the name that is above every name*" (Philippians 2:9).

Don't we want that too?

The Lord Jesus Christ gives his believers "*all things that pertain to life and godliness, through the knowledge of him who called us to his own glory and excellence*" (2 Peter 1:3). He gives us abundant grace to share the open door of the Gospel with others (1 Corinthians 16:9; 2 Corinthians 2:12; Colossians 4:2).

Look for an open door of ministry created just for you. It may be as small as visiting a lonely neighbor.

NO LUKEWARM HEARTS FOR JESUS!

REVELATION 3:14–22

How do you think the Christian church is doing in the present age? I tend to want to pat us on the back for all the good we are doing. The final church of the seven churches is Laodicea. If we put a historical age to these churches, this one represents the church from the 1900s to the present.

Laodicea was enormously wealthy and the banking center of that part of Asia Minor. It boasted a medical center that had developed an eye salve that was exported throughout the known world. The symbol of the Rod of Asclepius first appeared in Laodicea—a serpent-entwined rod wielded by the Greek god Asclepius, a deity associated with healing and medicine. This symbol is still used today to signify the art of medicine. This city was also known for the wool of black sheep that produced fine cloth known for its luxury. What they did not have was water. An aqueduct was run from the hot springs in Hierapolis, but by the time it arrived in Laodicea, the water was lukewarm. Another aqueduct ran from the cool mountain streams of Colossae, but by the time that water arrived, it too was lukewarm.

Due to this vulnerable water supply, the Laodiceans compromised with potential enemies to keep their water supply intact. They had wealth and prosperity, so these ancient people thought they were self-sufficient. Off the bat, we see that the Laodiceans were ready to compromise for their security and thought they could handle their issues without any help.

Jesus introduces himself to this final group of Christians.

> "And to the angel of the church in Laodicea write: 'The words of the Amen, the faithful and true witness, the beginning of God's creation.'" (3:14).

Jesus is the final Word, the authoritative Word. After He speaks, there is nothing else to say. His life is a witness of how we must approach the living God. Most importantly, Jesus rules all of God's creation, including Laodicea. They thought that they were self-sufficient, but they were not. Their pride smacks of the attitude we often see in America. We are a wealthy nation, our medical community is excellent, and we value fashion and material goods. At times we don't think we "need" God. But God sees through the façade.

> "I know your works: you are neither cold nor hot. Would that you were either cold or hot! So, because you are lukewarm, and neither hot nor cold, I will spit you out of my mouth. For you say, I am rich, I have prospered, and I need nothing, not realizing that you are wretched, pitiable, poor, blind, and naked" (3:15–17).

What are their positives? Does Jesus commend them?

First, he says that they think highly of themselves. They said, "*I am rich, I have prospered, and I need nothing.*" They thought they were self-sufficient, but Jesus smashes that lie. "*You are wretched, pitiable, poor, blind, and naked*" (3:17).

Notice how Jesus confronts them where they think they have it all together. Jesus asserts that they are poor, even though they think they are rich. He says they are blind, even though they are known for their curing salve. Finally, they are naked, though they think of themselves as the fashion capital of Asia Minor.

Like their water supply, Jesus says they are neither hot nor cold. They are lukewarm and nauseating—so much so that he will spit them out of his mouth (the Greek word here is *vomit*). The Laodicean church is reprimanded for compromising. Like their water supply, they are willing to compromise spiritually for comfort's sake. Their compromising spirit starts with emotional compromise, but slowly and surely moves to doctrinal compromise. The parishioners are not challenged, rebuked, or corrected. They are comfortable, and it makes Jesus sick. The word Laodicea means "rule of people." This church was not ruled by the Word of God but by the majority, not by the Lord Jesus but by the popular vote.

The Laodicean church was also complacent. As the popular expression goes, they were fat, dumb, and happy—and didn't really want it any other way. The Laodiceans measured themselves by the world's standards—and by that measure, they thought they looked pretty good. But Jesus measures them by his righteousness and calls them to be salt and light. A complacent church is neither.

But in our compromise, complacency, rebellion, and self-adulation, Jesus loves us! Like any good father, God disciplines those who belong to him (Deuteronomy 8:5; Proverbs 3:12). But he calls us to repent and turn to him. Our repentance starts with honest self-examination (Luke 18:9–14).

Jesus provides a way where there seems to be no way. Jesus does not want us to be ignorant or in the dark. He tells the Christians of Laodicea how to return to him

> "I counsel you to buy from me gold refined by fire, so that you may be rich, and white garments so that you may clothe yourself and the shame of your nakedness may not be seen, and salve to anoint your eyes, so that you may see" (3:18).

Jesus is always ready to come to our rescue.

"*Buy from me*" shows the church that Jesus is all they need. But buying denotes an exchange of one thing for another. However, the "Great Exchange" of the Christian life is that we get the righteousness that we need from Jesus, and he takes our sin upon himself.

> "For our sake he made him to be sin who knew no sin, so that in him we might become the righteousness of God" (2 Corinthians 5:21).

Jesus buys our freedom—freedom from our sin and the righteous wrath of God that we deserve. It enriches our lives and awakens our faith. He ransomed us with his precious blood!

> "...knowing that you were ransomed from the futile ways inherited from your forefathers, not with perishable things such as silver or gold, but with the precious blood of Christ, like that of a lamb without blemish or spot" (1 Peter 1:18–19).

We are all morally naked before the Lord God. None of us can achieve anything on our own merit. As we approach the throne, all our sin is exposed. But Jesus clothes us with purity and his righteousness.

We need spiritual clarity to navigate the complexities of life. The world will try to lead us astray like the Laodiceans. But in Jesus, we have 20/20 spiritual vision. "*The LORD opens the eyes of the blind...the LORD loves the righteous*" (Psalm 146:8).

> "Those whom I love, I reprove and discipline, so be zealous and repent. Behold, I stand at the door and knock. If anyone hears my voice and opens the door, I will come in to him and eat with him, and he with me" (3:19–20).

This verse was interpreted by William Holden Hunt in his painting, "Light of the World." Jesus is painted in his kingly garb and is knocking at the door that has been overgrown with weeds. Is Jesus knocking at your heart? Do you feel the Savior calling you to himself? It is time to say, "Yes, come into my heart, Lord Jesus." When we do, our lives will never be the same.

These overcomers will receive the greatest reward.

> "The one who conquers, I will grant him to sit with me on my throne, as I also conquered and sat down with my Father on his throne. He who has an ear, let him hear what the Spirit says to the churches" (3:21–22).

Open your ears to the Savior who calls you to repent and believe!

....
....
....
....
....
....
....
....
....
....
....
....
....
....

HEAVEN IS FOR REAL

REVELATION 4

Is heaven for real? Is it just a state of mind or a figment of the imagination created by men who don't want to die? We all want to know that heaven is real and what heaven looks like. It's funny, because if you ask a child to draw heaven, they can. They use bright yellow and gold, draw angel wings, and sometimes include a loved one who has died. They depict a joyful place of color and light.

> "After this I looked, and behold, a door standing open in heaven! And the first voice, which I had heard speaking to me like a trumpet, said, 'Come up here, and I will show you what must take place after this.' At once I was in the Spirit, and behold, a throne stood in heaven, with one seated on the throne. And he who sat there had the appearance of jasper and carnelian, and around the throne was a rainbow that had the appearance of an emerald" (4:1–3).

We see similar descriptions of the throne room in other books of the Bible (Isaiah 6; Daniel 7; Ezekiel 1).

Have you ever seen a light so brilliant and glorious that you felt you had caught a glimpse of God's glory? At times I have seen it during a sunrise or sunset—a bright, golden light on the edges of a cloud. The glory of heaven is so overwhelming that after he was on Mount Sinai with God, Moses glowed from his encounter.

> "Around the throne were twenty-four thrones, and seated on the thrones were twenty-four elders, clothed in white garments, with golden crowns on their heads. From the throne came flashes of lightning, and rumblings and peals of thunder, and before the throne were burning seven torches of fire, which are the seven spirits of God, and before the throne there was as it were a sea of glass, like crystal" (4:4–6).

Who do you think the twenty-four elders are? There are several possibilities. Jesus told his disciples, *"Truly, I say to you, in the new world, when the Son of Man will sit on his glorious throne, you who have followed me will also sit on twelve thrones, judging the twelve tribes of Israel"* (Matthew 19:28).

In our last lesson on the church of Laodicea, the overcomers were promised the right *"to sit with me [Jesus] on my throne, as I also conquered and sat down with my Father on his throne"* (3:21).

The seven spirits are the manifold fullness of the Holy Spirit, whose presence is with the Father and the Son.

> "And around the throne, on each side of the throne, are four living creatures, full of eyes in front and behind: the first living creature like a lion, the second living creature like an ox, the third living creature with the face of a man, and the fourth living creature like an eagle in flight. And the four living creatures, each of them with six wings, are full of eyes all around and within, and day and night they never cease to say, 'Holy, holy, holy, is the Lord God Almighty, who was and is and is to come!'" (4:6–8).

This same description is found in Ezekiel 1:4–14. What is the significance of the lion, the ox, the face of a man, and the eagle? Over the years, these symbols have come to represent the four Gospels.

The lion symbolizes the Gospel of Matthew, which was written to the Jews, where Jesus is depicted as the Lion of the tribe of Judah. A lion is the powerful king of the animal kingdom, symbolizing that Jesus is the King of kings.

The ox symbolizes the Gospel of Mark (some theologians think it is Luke). The ox was a domesticated animal whose great strength served man. Jesus came to serve mankind; he is the Suffering Servant.

The image of a man stands for Luke's Gospel, which spoke of the humanity of Jesus. Finally, the Gospel of John is symbolized by an eagle, the only bird that can stare directly into the sun and not be blinded. This Gospel focuses on the majesty and deity of Jesus.

Jesus made it clear to his disciples—and he makes it clear to us—that we are to serve others in humility and love just as he did. Do you know someone that needs care? Are you willing to serve that person in the name of Jesus?

> "And whenever the living creatures give glory and honor and thanks to him who is seated on the throne, who lives forever and ever, the twenty-four elders fall down before him who is seated on the throne and worship

him who lives forever and ever. They cast their crowns before the throne, saying, 'Worthy are you, our Lord and God, to receive glory and honor and power, for you created all things, and by your will they existed and were created'" (4:9–11).

Notice the response of those who sit on the thrones. They give their crowns to the one who sits on the throne. Whatever our calling may be for the kingdom of God, our success is due only to the Lord's hand on us. Jesus is the only one who is worthy to wear a crown.

Billy Graham, arguably the greatest evangelist of the twentieth century, wrote an autobiography about his life called *Just As I Am*. In this book, he gives the Lord Jesus all the credit for his ministry. Graham simply said yes to his calling, and he was led step-by-step to build the kingdom of God.[1]

All of us are called to serve God. Only some of us say yes. Whether we preach the Gospel to thousands or pray with patients in one small-town hospital, our acts of faithful service are equally important in God's kingdom. What is God calling you to do? When you respond, there is a crown in store for you—a crown that belongs to Jesus, and you will lay it at his feet (4:10).

How can we know that heaven is real? How can we be sure that God's promise of eternity is true?

> "So when God desired to show more convincingly to the heirs of the promise the unchangeable character of his purpose, he guaranteed it with an oath, so that by two unchangeable things, in which it is impossible for God to lie, we who have fled for refuge might have strong encouragement to hold fast to the hope set before us. We have this as a sure and steadfast anchor of the soul, a hope that enters into the inner place behind the curtain, where Jesus has gone as a forerunner on our behalf" (Hebrews 6:17–20).

The Lord Jesus Christ has gone before us. God has promised, and God does not lie. Christ died and rose again, and everyone who believes in him receives eternal life (John 3:15–16).

---

1   Billy Graham, *Just As I Am* (New York: HarperCollins, 1973).

WEEK

3

BEHIND THE VEIL...
HEAVEN IS FOR REAL

DAY 11

BEHOLD
THE LAMB

REVELATION 5

As we study Revelation, we will be in the throne room for quite a while. There is a lot of action happening there—it is not boring! As we proceed, we need to remember that God exists outside of how we record time. He counts time differently than we do (2 Peter 3:8). In our earthly nature, while we are caught in the cycle of times and seasons and calendars, it is difficult for us to understand God's eternal nature. But this passage reminds us that God is eternal, and so is heaven.

In Revelation 5, something earth-shaking is about to happen. This is the moment that all creation has been waiting for—the time for Jesus to take his rightful place in God's kingdom.

> "Then I saw in the right hand of him who was seated on the throne a scroll written within and on the back, sealed with seven seals" (5:1).

What is the scroll? We get more information in Daniel 12:1–4. The opening of the scroll seems to kickstart the beginning of the reign of Jesus on earth.

All creation is holding its collective breath to see who is worthy to unseal the scroll.

> "And I saw a mighty angel proclaiming with a loud voice, 'Who is worthy to open the scroll and break its seals?' And no one in heaven or on earth or under the earth was able to open the scroll or to look into it, and I began to weep loudly because no one was found worthy to open the scroll or to look into it. And one of the elders said to me, 'Weep no more; behold, the Lion of the tribe of Judah, the Root of David, has conquered, so that he can open the scroll and its seven seals.' And between the throne and the four living creatures and among the elders I saw a Lamb standing, as though it had been slain, with seven horns and with seven eyes, which are the seven spirits of God sent out into all the earth. And he went and took the scroll from the right hand of him who was seated on the throne" (5:2–7).

John knew that opening the scroll was a good thing—that is why he wept, thinking no one was worthy. I don't know about you, but I would expect a strong beast like a lion, or a mighty warrior like King David, to have the power to open this important scroll.

But it's a lamb—and not only a lamb, but one damaged and slain. A lamb has no natural defense; they are helpless animals. Why a lamb? This reference takes us back to Exodus and the first Passover.

> "For I will pass through the land of Egypt that night, and I will strike all the firstborn in the land of Egypt, both man and beast; and on all the gods of Egypt I will execute judgments: I am the LORD. The blood shall be a sign for you, on the houses where you are. And when I see the blood, I will pass over you, and no plague will befall you to destroy you, when I strike the land of Egypt" (Exodus 12:12–13).

Jesus is the personification of the Passover lamb that saved the Jewish people from the judgment of death that was falling on Egypt. Jesus died on Passover as the perfect, spotless Lamb of God. So here in Revelation 5, we see not Jesus the King of kings or Jesus, the High Priest that can open the scroll—but the sacrificial Jesus, the Lamb of God who willingly gave his life for the world.

> *"And when he had taken the scroll, the four living creatures and the twenty-four elders fell down before the Lamb, each holding a harp, and golden bowls full of incense, which are the prayers of the saints. And they sang a new song, saying, 'Worthy are you to take the scroll and to open its seals, for you were slain, and by your blood you ransomed people for God from every tribe and language and people and nation, and you have made them a kingdom and priests to our God, and they shall reign on the earth. Then I looked, and I heard around the throne and the living creatures and the elders the voice of many angels, numbering myriads of myriads and thousands of thousands, saying with a loud voice, 'Worthy is the Lamb who was slain, to receive power and wealth and wisdom and might and honor and glory and blessing!' And I heard every creature in heaven and on earth and under the earth and in the sea, and all that is in them, saying, 'To him who sits on the throne and to the Lamb be blessing and honor and glory and might forever and ever!' And the four living creatures said, 'Amen!' and the elders fell down and worshiped"* (5:8–14).

This is what heaven is like—worship. Have you ever been in church, singing or praying, and felt an overpowering love? That is what true worship feels like, as we worship the eternal God in *"spirit and in truth"* (John 4:24). The one we praise is Jesus, the slain Lamb who willingly died so to purchase us for God, that we might glorify the Father and the Son forever. All praise to the Lamb!

....

....

....

....

....

....

....

....

....

....

....

....

....

....

....

....

....

....

....

....

....

OVERVIEW OF THE TRIBULATION

REVELATION 6:1-2

Is heaven for real? According to Revelation, it is. The Old Testament prophets also speak of the glory of heaven, particularly in Ezekiel 1. Jesus declares to the thief beside him on the cross that *"today you will be with me in paradise"* (Luke 23:43).

Jesus also spoke of "the end" of the earth. *"But the one who endures to the end will be saved. And this gospel of the kingdom will be proclaimed throughout the whole world as a testimony to all nations, and then the end will come"* (Matthew 24:13–14).

What is the end? Scripture gives us snapshots of the dreadful day of the Lord. *"But the day of the Lord will come like a thief, and then the heavens will pass away with a roar, and the heavenly bodies will be burned up and dissolved, and the earth and the works that are done on it will be exposed. ...But according to his promise we are waiting for new heavens and a new earth in which righteousness dwells"* (2 Peter 3:10, 13).

Revelation 6 is a snapshot of what is to come. In later chapters, we will describe these events in more detail. As we read these verses, we need to remember that it is Jesus, the Lamb who died for us, who allows the seals to be broken. The scroll brings forth the new heaven and new earth, but first, a time of tribulation occurs.

When I was a child, I used to have nightmares. I would wake up crying, go into my mom and dad's room, and crawl into bed with them. I needed that security. Chapter 6 of Revelation reminds me of my nightmares. This chapter is full of difficult, traumatic events: death, destruction, famine, and fighting. No human has control over these supernatural events.

We have learned that only the Lamb of God was worthy to open the sealed scroll. This scroll contained the history and destiny of mankind and creation—God's ultimate plan for his creation. The one worthy to open the scroll is the one who came to save.

The six seals are an outline of the time of tribulation. We will see a more in-depth description from this point in chapter 6 until chapter 19. The judgments will appear from different points of view. From the book of Daniel, we know that there will be a seven-year period when the world will experience the tribulation, the judgment of God. In the middle of the seven years, there will be a revealing of blasphemy and ungodliness like the world has never seen. Persecution of Christians will be at its height, and for three and a half years, all hell will break loose against God's people, Jews, and Christians alike. At the end of the seven years, Jesus will come in his glory—not as a humble servant riding on a donkey, but as a mighty warrior riding on a horse. This will end the reign of the Antichrist and begin the reign of Jesus on earth, where all knees will bow on the earth, under the earth, and in heaven (Philippians 2:10–11).

At this point in Revelation, John is still in the throne room of God, the place of God's amazing glory (4:1–11). As you read these verses, do not forget that glory. God is in control.

In the first four seals, it is those weird living creatures—the lion, the ox, the man, and the eagle that summon what we call the "Four Horsemen" of the Apocalypse. Interestingly, these horrific catastrophes are in the same order that Jesus mentioned in Matthew 24 when speaking about his return.

> "Now I watched when the Lamb opened one of the seven seals, and I heard one of the four living creatures say with a voice like thunder, "Come!" And I looked, and behold, a white horse! And its rider had a bow, and a crown was given to him, and he came out conquering, and to conquer" (6:1–2).

The first seal opened by the Lamb is a white horse carrying a bow but no arrows. He was given a crown and *"came out conquering and to conquer"* (6:2). This has an eerie resemblance to Revelation 19, when Jesus returns as the warrior. But it is not Jesus; it is a counterfeit, the Antichrist. He will bear a resemblance to Jesus and say similar things as Jesus, but his coming instead will bring war, famine, and death, not peace.

Some have said that there is an antichrist in each generation. Paul wrote of a similar theme, saying that the *"man of lawlessness"* will come when Jesus returns, even though the spirit of this *"lawlessness is already at work"* (2 Thessalonians 2:3–7). John wrote about this theme as well. *"Every spirit that does not confess Jesus is not from God. This is the spirit of the antichrist, which you heard was coming and now is in the world already*" (1 John 4:3; see also 1 John 2:18; 2 John 1:7). By this definition, Adolf Hitler would have qualified, as would Joseph Stalin. Their hatred for the Jews was contagious to an entire group of people.

We can easily become unsettled when we see evil like this in history and the present. Paul wrote to encourage us to set aside this anxiety:

> "Now concerning the coming of our Lord Jesus Christ and our being gathered together to him, we ask you, brothers, not to be quickly shaken in mind or alarmed, either by a spirit or a spoken word, or a letter seeming to be from us, to the effect that the day of the Lord has come. Let no one deceive you in any way. For that day will not come, unless the rebellion comes first, and the man of lawlessness is revealed, the son of destruction, who opposes and exalts himself against every so-called god or object of worship, so that he takes his seat in the temple of God, proclaiming himself to be God" (2 Thessalonians 2:1–4).

Sometimes it feels like the man of lawlessness is being empowered by Satan. But God is in control! Paul continues:

> "*Do you not remember that when I was still with you I told you these things? And you know what is restraining him now so that he may be revealed in his time. For the mystery of lawlessness is already at work. Only he who now restrains it will do so until he is out of the way*" (2 Thessalonians 2:5–7).

There seems to be a restraining power throughout history. I believe the restrainer is the Holy Spirit in the lives of Christians. This horseman is bent on conquest, and Satan wants to take worship away from God the Father. The enemy uses deceit, lies, and manipulation to entice people away from the living God. He doesn't have to use "arrows" as weapons, just threats. But in the time of tribulation, God takes his reins off Satan and lets him have his way until the climax of deceit.

But take heart. Jesus wins, for his power is far greater than Satan (2 Thessalonians 2:8–9).

So when you watch the evening news, don't grow anxious. Jesus gives peace through his Spirit—a peace that cannot be taken away, no matter what is going on in the world. "*Peace I leave with you; my peace I give to you. Not as the world gives do I give to you. Let not your hearts be troubled, neither let them be afraid*" (John 14:27).

SLAUGHTER, FAMINE, AND "I WANT OUTTA HERE"

REVELATION 6:3–8

The first seal of judgment has been opened, and we see the Four Horsemen of the Apocalypse. The first horseman symbolizes the arrival of the Antichrist, who desires to take the entire world under his control.

The second seal is opened.

> "When he opened the second seal, I heard the second living creature say, 'Come!' And out came another horse, bright red. Its rider was permitted to take peace from the earth, so that people should slay one another, and he was given a great sword" (6:3–4).

In the first seal, the Antichrist has no arrows, which signifies his conquering with intrigue, not a sword. But after the second seal, this rider carries a large sword, to make people "*slay one another.*"

The Greek word used here for "*slay*" means slaughter, unrestrained murder, and no civil control. If this doesn't seem possible, think about world history.

Hitler's Germany killed more than ten million people who endured horrific treatment as Holocaust victims. The Hutu tribe massacred nearly a million people from the Tutsi tribe during the Rwandan genocide in 1994. *Left to Tell* is a poignant book of one young woman's spiritual journey through that hundred-day dark time. The Terror Famine in Ukraine, starting in 1932 through the evil of Joseph Stalin, is estimated to have killed 1.5 to 7 million people. Japanese Imperial forces slaughtered 500,000 Chinese people during the Nanking Massacre in 1937. Mao Zedong's "Great Leap Forward" policies killed more than 45 million people through murder and starvation between 1958 and 1962. Between 1975 and 1979, the Khmer Rouge killed nearly two million people during the Cambodian genocide. The Srebrenica massacre in 1995 killed more than 8,000 Bosniak Muslims. All of these overwhelming tragedies are part of our recent history, terrible evidence of man slaughtering man. As we move towards the end times, abominations like these will be prevalent.

The third seal is announced.

> "When he opened the third seal, I heard the third living creature say, 'Come!' And I looked, and behold, a black horse! And its rider had a pair of scales in his hand. And I heard what seemed to be a voice in the midst of the four living creatures, saying, 'A quart of wheat for a denarius, and three quarts of barley for a denarius, and do not harm the oil and wine!'" (6:5–6).

What is the meaning of this third seal? *"A quart of wheat for a denarius, and three quarts of barley for a denarius"* means that one day's wage would only pay for food for one person. Barley was considered a lesser foodstuff, but it would feed a small family with nothing left over for the other necessities of life. Economic catastrophe has brought famine to the people. Notice, however, that the oil and wine are untouched. The rich can still afford these luxury items, but the poor can barely afford basic sustenance. One historical illustration of this economic chaos happened in Germany after the First World War. Due to out-of-control inflation, people said that a wheelbarrow of cash bought one loaf of bread. Then the government set rigid controls on buying and selling, and these difficult times led to the rise and ultimate control of the Third Reich. A similar dynamic is played out later in the tribulation, as the Antichrist gains more and more power. But God is in control!

The fourth seal is announced.

> "When he opened the fourth seal, I heard the voice of the fourth living creature say, 'Come!' And I looked, and behold, a pale horse! And its rider's name was Death, and Hades followed him. And they were given authority over a fourth of the earth, to kill with sword and with famine and with pestilence and by wild beasts of the earth" (6:7–8).

The fourth seal is opened again by the Lamb. The horse is pale, translated from the Greek word *chloros,* where we get the word chlorine. This pale, sickly horse was death, with Hades following close behind. Death takes the body, and Hades takes the soul. The passage seems to match what Jesus claimed in Matthew 24, that *"nation will rise against nation, and kingdom against kingdom, and there will be famines and earthquakes in various places. All these are but the beginning of the birth pains"* (Matthew 24:7–8).

This final horseman has the power to kill a fourth of the population by sword, famine, plague, and wild beasts. If more than 7.7 billion people live on earth, and a fourth of them are killed, then almost 2 billion people die. By comparison, the population of the United States is 330 million, the population of India is 1.3 billion, and the population of China is 1.3 billion.

So, the four living creatures who stand before the throne of God and praise him 24/7 announce the opening of the seals. With each seal, they say, "*Come.*" They aren't talking to John; he is already there. I believe they are speaking to the only one who can stop the madness—Jesus, the returning Messiah. Come, Lord Jesus, come in your power and might. Come!

That is what we need to be saying, too. Come, Lord Jesus. Only through his presence will the ordeal of the dreaded Day of the Lord come to an end.

Are you in a season of suffering? Does it feel like all is lost in your life? Then call the Lord Jesus to come, the Lord Jesus who said, "*I am the resurrection and the life. Whoever believes in me, though he die, yet shall he live, and everyone who lives and believes in me shall never die. Do you believe this?*" (John 11:25–26).

MARTYRS AND THE UNREPENTANT

REVELATION 6:9–17

Remember, chapter 6 outlines what is to come in future chapters. It is a forewarning to John about the revelations that will come into greater focus.

The Four Horsemen of the Apocalypse bring different levels of destruction. Each of them represented a seal of judgment. When we get to the fifth seal, the focus changes from the earth to the heavenly realm.

The first four seals speak about earthy things; the last three speak of heavenly realities that coincide with them.

> "When he opened the fifth seal, I saw under the altar the souls of those who had been slain for the word of God and for the witness they had borne. They cried out with a loud voice, 'O Sovereign Lord, holy and true, how long before you will judge and avenge our blood on those who dwell on the earth?' Then they were each given a white robe and told to rest a little longer, until the number of their fellow servants and their brothers should be complete, who were to be killed as they themselves had been" (6:9–11).

With the fifth seal, notice that the Lamb isn't mentioned. The verse simply says, "*he opened.*" But Jesus is still in control. The seals show us a reality in heaven that we are allowed to observe. First is the fate of the martyrs.

The first martyr for Jesus was Stephen, recorded in Acts 7. As he died, he cried out, "*Lord, do not hold this sin against them*" (Acts 7:60). Similar words were spoken by Jesus when he said from the cross, "*Father forgive them, for they know not what they do*" (Luke 23:34). God commands us to forgive, for vengeance is his (Deuteronomy 32:35; Romans 12:19; Hebrews 10:30). This passage refers to the martyrs killed during the tribulation. Judgment is now being passed out, and these martyrs reflect that. They call for vengeance, but they must wait because their full number is not complete.

Living in the United States, we may seem immune to martyrdom. Yet the statistics are clear. More people have died for the Christian faith in the twentieth century than in any other era. Martyrs are still being added to the roll call of the faithful. It is estimated that 100,000 Christians die each year for their faith. According to some sources, this number may be an exaggeration, but 10,000 each year is not. Church bombings are common in other countries, and we have recently seen persecution in Texas.

Why does this happen? We live in a world of sin and darkness. When Jesus first came, he brought light into that darkness. Since then, the forces of darkness have been waging war against the forces of God.

As Christians, we are all called into battle, but we know who wins the war! See Ephesians 6:10–11.

We must stand up for our faith so that the world will see what true faith in Jesus looks like. Has there been a time in your life when you should have stood up for Jesus, but you sat down instead? Your response is natural. But God gives supernatural grace (James 4:6). Peter denied Jesus three times, and all the disciples fell asleep when Jesus asked for their fellowship and prayer in the garden of Gethsemane.

Only the Lord's strength can give us the courage we need to stand up for the Lord Jesus and be counted as His.

The sixth seal is opened.

....

....

....

....

....

....

....

....

WHO CAN STAND?

REVELATION 7

The apostle John has been given a dreadful overview of the tribulation, so fearful that the kings of the earth call to the mountains to hide them from God's wrath:

> "Then the kings of the earth and the great ones and the generals and the rich and the powerful, and everyone, slave and free, hid themselves in the caves and among the rocks of the mountains, calling to the mountains and rocks, 'Fall on us and hide us from the face of him who is seated on the throne, and from the wrath of the Lamb, for the great day of their wrath has come, and who can stand?'" (6:15–17).

When the going gets tough, who can stand firm? The answer is in chapter 7.

> "After this, I saw four angels standing at the four corners of the earth, holding back the four winds of the earth, that no wind might blow on earth or sea or against any tree. Then I saw another angel ascending from the rising of the sun, with the seal of the living God, and he called with a loud voice to the four angels who had been given power to harm earth and sea, saying, 'Do not harm the earth or the sea or the trees, until we have sealed the servants of our God on their foreheads'" (7:1–3).

Despite the coming judgment that God has ordained, he makes sure that those who believe in him will be protected.

Chapter 7 is a vision into the heavenly realms—a heavenly reality to what is transpiring on earth. It begins with four powerful angels holding back the four winds, representing the tumultuous events we just outlined. A fifth angel appears to proclaim that a seal is needed as some form of protection from the wrath of God to come. We see other references to a seal in Ephesians 1:13 and 2 Corinthians 1:21–22.

The seal is the presence of the Holy Spirit promised to those who believe in Jesus Christ. The Holy Spirit gives those who follow Jesus the ability to hear his voice, respond to his call, and be strengthened in our inner being for whatever comes our way.

What follows is a very Jewish listing of the twelve tribes of Israel—numbering 144,000, with each tribe contributing 12,000. Some theologians believe that at the end times, God will touch the hearts of those Jews who have not yet believed in the reality that Jesus is their Messiah. These 144,000 will have a special anointing to go out during the tribulation and bring in a great harvest of souls. Another thought is that the number twelve symbolizes complete fulfillment. The book of Revelation alone has twenty-two occurrences of the number twelve.

The next multitude, mentioned in verses 9 and 10, are those who, through their ministry, come to faith in Jesus; these are Jews and Gentiles alike. The palm branches take us back to the first Palm Sunday, when Jesus entered Jerusalem over two thousand years ago, to shouts of "*Hosanna, blessed is he who comes in the name of the Lord*" (Mark 11:9). These same Jews shouted five days later, "*Crucify him!*" (Mark 15:13–14). At his second coming, Jesus will be accepted as the Messiah by all tribes, nations, and peoples. This multitude has come out of the great tribulation and washed their robes in the blood of the Lamb.

This multitude praises Jesus, the Lamb of God. As you read through the rest of the verses in Revelation 7, you get the sense that all has been made right. God has been faithful. What a glorious scene! We are made to worship the God who created us. When you go to church, do you expect to "get" something or to "give" something? The church was not established to entertain; it was established to worship God. That is what we see in these verses. Those who went through the horrors of the end times are full of worship, and they show it.

> "*Therefore they are before the throne of God, and serve him day and night in his temple; and he who sits on the throne will shelter them with his presence. They shall hunger no more, neither thirst anymore; the sun shall not strike them, nor any scorching heat. For the Lamb in the midst of the throne will be their shepherd, and he will guide them to springs of living water, and God will wipe away every tear from their eyes*" (7:15–17).

All those who wash their clothes in the blood of the Lamb are led into the throne room. God spreads his tent over them. They are in his presence and are part of his people. Hunger, thirst, and heat will no longer haunt them.

The Lamb will be their Shepherd, leader, guide, and protector. "*God will wipe away every tear from their eyes*" (7:17). We will see this again at the end of Revelation. This vision is a fast-forward to the exhortation to the seven churches—not to give up amidst persecution. I love the fact that God steps down from his throne to perform such an intimate and tender act as wiping away the tears of his people.

Thousands of years before, the psalmist felt the sting of tears: "*My tears have been my food day and night, while they say to me all the day long, 'Where is your God?'*" (Psalm 42:3). In distress, he strengthened his heart in God, trusting the Lord for salvation. "*Why are you cast down, O my soul, and why are you in turmoil within me? Hope in God; for I shall again praise him, my salvation and my God*" (Psalm 42:11).

This passage is a promise to each of us who believe in Jesus. God has not forgotten. He moves his angelic force, his Son, and his Spirit to protect his people. Who will be able to stand up to the wrath of God? Those who know Jesus as their Lamb and Shepherd, their Redeemer and Savior.

WEEK

4

WHO CAN STAND UNDER GOD'S JUDGMENTS?

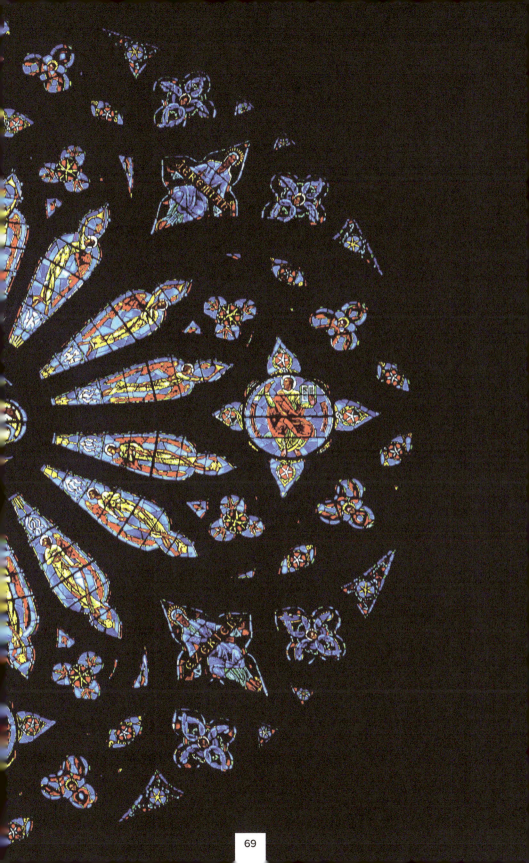

THE POWER OF PRAYER

REVELATION 8

The opening of the seventh and final seal of judgment takes us back to the throne room and the heavenly realities. As the seventh seal is broken, it seems to inaugurate the next set of seven trumpet judgments. But first, God wants us to see something important.

> "When the Lamb opened the seventh seal, there was silence in heaven for about half an hour. Then I saw the seven angels who stand before God, and seven trumpets were given to them. And another angel came and stood at the altar with a golden censer, and he was given much incense to offer with the prayers of all the saints on the golden altar before the throne, and the smoke of the incense, with the prayers of the saints, rose before God from the hand of the angel. Then the angel took the censer and filled it with fire from the altar and threw it on the earth, and there were peals of thunder, rumblings, flashes of lightning, and an earthquake. Now the seven angels who had the seven trumpets prepared to blow them" (8:1–6).

We have seen that in the throne room of God, there is 24/7 adoration and worship. But now, at the opening of the seventh seal, there is silence for about half an hour. I call this pregnant silence, where you know something wonderful, important, and critical is about to occur.

In the first six chapters, the seals of judgment seem to outline the final days to come. But before the onset of the final judgments, the worship of God is replaced by silence. I think this passage shows how our prayers are critical to the heavenly realities. God can do his work without mankind, but he chooses to have his people play a role in the heavenly drama. Are the prayers of God's people demanding judgment? Are the prayers begging for God to make our broken world right again? The censer of prayers combined with the fire of judgment is hurled to the earth. God is moving to set the world right.

When I think of the Holocaust victims during Nazi Germany, I wonder: Did they pray for justice? For vengeance? For the world to be put right again? Possibly. When I consider the Tutsi tribe in Rwanda, did the believers pray for justice, for God to move against the Hutu tribe that persecuted them? Throughout history—during the Terror Famine in Ukraine, the Mao Zedong Massacre in China, and the Srebrenica Massacre in Bosnia—did believers cry out for God's justice?

The rest of Revelation 8 announces the beginning of the trumpet judgments. At first glance, these trumpet judgments look terrifying—and they are. But we have also studied similar judgments in the book of Exodus. In Revelation 5, at the opening of the fifth seal, the martyrs under the altar are praying for God to avenge their lives. We saw a similar request of God's people in Exodus 3:7–8, *"Then the LORD said, 'I have surely seen the affliction of my people who are in Egypt and have heard their cry because of their taskmasters. I know their sufferings, and I have come down to deliver them...'"* This passage begins a series of plagues on Pharaoh and Egypt.

Notice that God puts limits on these catastrophic events: only *"a third of the earth was burned up"* (8:7). Will these events really happen? Maybe so, but remember, God's people have the seal of ownership and protection. Catastrophic events happen in our world today, but as we will see in future chapters, God has a reason to use judgment. That reason is love.

This all seems horrific, but look what Jesus foretold, *"And there will be signs in sun and moon and stars, and on the earth distress of nations in perplexity because of the roaring of the sea and the waves, people fainting with fear and with foreboding of what is coming on the world. For the powers of the heavens will be shaken. And then they will see the Son of Man coming in a cloud with power and great glory. Now when these things begin to take place, straighten up and raise your heads, because your redemption is drawing near"* (Luke 21:25–28). In other words, when it seems like all hell is breaking loose, that is the time when Jesus will return.

We live in a world where bad things happen, because we live in a world where evil exists. But sometimes, when our lives are the most tumultuous, our suffering draws us closer to the Lord God (Romans 5:3–5).

As Christians, do we do all that we can to alleviate the evils of this world? I know that you may be like me, thinking, "What can I do? I'm here in the United States, and I have no power." Wrong. We always have the power of prayer. *"For though we walk in the flesh, we are not waging war according to the flesh. For the weapons of our warfare are not of the flesh but have divine power to destroy strongholds. We destroy arguments and every lofty opinion raised against the knowledge of God, and take every thought captive to obey Christ"* (2 Corinthians 10:3–5).

Our prayers matter. The prayers of the ancient Jews did, and so do ours.

WOE IS ME!

REVELATION 9

At this point, the judgments of the first four seals have affected man indirectly. The essentials of food, water, daylight, and daily rhythms are compromised. But the last three trumpet judgments now affect man personally and have supernatural, heavenly elements.

The last three trumpet judgments are called the "woe judgments."

The fifth trumpet is a heavenly unleashing of the Abyss. We hear about the Abyss when Jesus drove the legion of demons out of the demonically possessed man (see Luke 8:26–39). Those demons knew exactly who Jesus was, the "*Son of the Most High God*," and they begged not to be thrown into the Abyss. Jesus granted their request and put them into a herd of pigs who subsequently drowned. The Abyss is so bad, even the demons don't want to go there. But God is in control of the Abyss. "*For if God did not spare angels when they sinned, but cast them into hell and committed them to chains of gloomy darkness to be kept until the judgment*" (2 Peter 2:4; see also Jude 6).

What emerges from the Abyss are locust-like creatures who are under God's control. Are they really locusts? Probably not, since there is a king called Abaddon or Apollyon, which means destruction. Locusts in the natural world devour everything green in their path, yet these locust-like creatures must leave all green things alone. Instead, they are commanded to torture those humans who do not have the seal of God on their foreheads. Their torture is like a scorpion bite, horribly painful but not lethal. Notice they are only to have this power for five months. Again, God puts limits on these demonic creatures. His mercy urges people who still refuse his offer of love to repent and turn to him.

The sixth trumpet judgment is equally bizarre, supernatural, and scary. What does the Euphrates River have to do with anything? It was the location of ancient Babylon, an enemy of the Hebrews. It was also the boundary of ancient Rome, who always kept a watchful eye on the land beyond the Euphrates for barbaric hordes. It was where the mighty Assyrian nation originated that conquered the northern kingdom of Israel. It represents the enemy of God's people.

Notice that God releases the angels who release the 200 million troops to kill one-third of mankind. Are these troops really demonic beings, or do these images represent helicopters, military tanks, or future weapons of mass destruction? Are they symbolic of the multitude of evil within mankind who refuse the living God, who worship demons and idols? Those who murder at will, practice sorcery, steal, and engage in sexual immorality (9:20–21)? Three plagues of fire, sulfur, and smoke are unleashed—yet look at the reaction: "*The rest of mankind, who were not killed by these plagues, did not repent of the works of their hands nor give up worshiping demons and idols of gold and silver and bronze and stone and wood, which cannot see or hear or walk*" (9:20).

Whatever the reality of these judgments, God is in control. He puts a limit on all this destruction: only one-third. God's goal for these wayward men and women, who still carry within themselves the image of God, is to bring them to repentance and salvation.

God's will is that no one would perish but that all would come to the saving grace of his Son, Jesus. God will woo us and draw us, but if we still refuse the love of Jesus, he will try to save the wayward ones with judgment. That is what we are seeing in these verses—a Father whose kindness in patience is meant to lead all to repentance (Romans 2:4–5).

At this point in the book of Revelation, we become aware of that characteristic of God we don't like to embrace—his judgment. So many times, we think of God as a glorified Santa Claus—a gift-giver who hears our requests, a grandfather that loves us unconditionally. He is all that, but he is also a God who will not allow evil to go unchecked—either in our lives or in the world. He is a God of judgment.

Lest we forget, God protected the ancient Israelites from the most horrific plagues he brought on Egypt. The blood of the Passover Lamb, applied to the doorposts of the Israelites' homes, protected the ancient Jews from the angel of death. The blood of the Lamb, Jesus, will protect us from the wrath and judgments of God. Woe is me? Not eternally! I can lift my hands in worship to the Lamb, even in the tumultuous waves of an uncertain world.

THE GOOD, THE BAD, AND THE UGLY

REVELATION 10 AND 11

In chapter 10, we get an intermission. It's as if the Lord knew that all these visions would be overwhelming to John and his readers. What follows is a description of a mighty angel, with similarities to the vision of Jesus in chapter 1. He plants one foot on the land and one on the sea—symbolizing his authority over all sea and land. He roars like a lion and swears by God the Father—two qualities that make me think that he is Jesus, the Lion of Judah. He proclaims that time is up. The seventh trumpet is the announcement of the return of Jesus. *"But that in the days of the trumpet call to be sounded by the seventh angel, the mystery of God would be fulfilled, just as he announced to his servants the prophets"* (10:7). What mystery? *"Lest you be wise in your own sight, I do not want you to be unaware of this mystery, brothers: a partial hardening has come upon Israel, until the fullness of the Gentiles has come in"* (Romans 11:25).

We see the same idea in Ephesians 3:6–10: *"This mystery is that the Gentiles are fellow heirs, members of the same body, and partakers of the promise in Christ Jesus through the gospel. Of this gospel I was made a minister according to the gift of God's grace, which was given me by the working of his power. To me, though I am the very least of all the saints, this grace was given, to preach to the Gentiles the unsearchable riches of Christ, and to bring to light for everyone what is the plan of the mystery hidden for ages in God, who created all things, so that through the church the manifold wisdom of God might now be made known to the rulers and authorities in the heavenly places."*

Colossians 1:26–27 speaks of this theme as well: *"...the mystery hidden for ages and generations but now revealed to his saints. To them God chose to make known how great among the Gentiles are the riches of the glory of this mystery, which is Christ in you, the hope of glory."* So, this announcement seems to proclaim that the mystery is fulfilled. The full number of Gentiles has come in; the work of the church is complete.

This little scroll, not to be confused with the scroll we have been unrolling, is to be eaten, taken in, and digested. It is sweet at first but soon becomes sour in the stomach. This same scenario happened to Ezekiel, who was commanded to eat God's words about judgment (Ezekiel 3:1–3). The sweetness is the reality that God will now set all things right. The evils that permeate our world will no longer plague his people. The sourness is the reality that judgment will be severe for those who refuse God. The reality of judgment should bring sadness and sourness to the hearts of believers.

John is told to prophesy again, and his prophecy is recorded in Revelation 11–14. In these verses, God explains who the players are in this final drama.

The focus is Jerusalem, God's Holy City. We know that Jerusalem has been sacked by enemies and rebuilt many times over the years. If this prophecy in Revelation is actual, it will happen again and last for forty-two months, or three and a half years, or 1,260 days. While Jerusalem is in the throes of fighting, two witnesses will be empowered by God with miraculous powers, like Moses and Elijah of the Old Testament. No one will be able to overcome them until God's perfect timing, when He permits the beast of the Abyss, the Antichrist, to kill them. Notice the reaction of the people. Their expressions of joy become like a pseudo-Christmas party, as they exchange gifts to celebrate. They lie exposed in Jerusalem for three and a half days, then come back to life by God's breath and are taken to heaven in view of all.

After this, one-tenth of Jerusalem collapses. Seven thousand souls are killed, and the people realize they are dealing with the Most High God.

What does it take for people to bow to our Creator God? For some, faith comes easily; for others, it is a struggle. God is thundering from heaven and bringing miraculous signs and wonders to convince those who refuse him. If the love of Jesus on the cross doesn't draw someone, then God uses his judgments of wrath. Like in the times of Noah, he waits. Three and a half years of horrific times are designed to convince even the most hardened heart to repent.

The final seventh trumpet sounds and time is up. The reign of Jesus begins where his followers are rewarded *"for destroying those who destroy the earth."* Notice that there is no middle ground—you either believe in the Holy God, or you turn away to your destruction. By this time, those who turn from God will sink deeper and deeper into sin and degradation.

With the appearance of Jesus and the opening of God's temple in heaven, an old element of God's glory reappears, the ark of the covenant. This was the same ark that Joshua carried while his forces encircled Jericho. On the seventh day, the sound of trumpets and the call of the people broke down the walls of that fortified city, opening the way for God's people to enter the promised land.

This triumphal entry will happen again, but this time, the Commander is Jesus, the army is composed of believers, and the promised land is heaven.

LOOKS LIKE A MELODRAMA TO ME

REVELATION 12

God loves to draw his people to himself. His passion is that they recognize him as the one true God, as Yahweh (the ancient Hebrew name for God), and as the great I AM (the God who was and is and is to come). But mighty forces fight against the fellowship of God and man.

At this point in Revelation, we have many questions. Why does God go to such lengths to save wayward people? Why doesn't God just let them go? Chapters 12 and 13 answer that question.

First, there are several more players to identify.

In verse 1, a sign appears in heaven: "*a woman clothed with the sun, with the moon under her feet, and on her head a crown of twelve stars.*" Roman Catholics believe that this woman is Mary, the mother of Jesus. However, most theologians believe that she represents the nation of Israel.

The nasty red dragon with seven heads, ten horns, and seven crowns is Satan. His horns signify that his power is great, and he desires the kingship of all he encounters.

The male child who will rule with an iron scepter is Jesus.

So, Satan wants to devour Jesus before he even grows up. And he almost succeeded when King Herod sent out his troops to kill all male babies two years old and younger. The beginning of Jesus's life and ascension is recounted in verse 5. But Satan did not have his way with Jesus. Remember, the cross was part of God's sovereign plan. Satan may have thought he had won, but the cross spelled his defeat.

The next player we meet is Michael, the archangel. According to Daniel, he seems to have a special assignment with Israel. There is much debate about this angelic battle—does it take place in the future, or has it already taken place at the fall of Satan that is recorded in Ezekiel? Through the book of Job and various other Scriptures, we know that Satan is in the heavenly realms and is accusing God's people before the throne day and night. So, is this a battle that will take place as we draw near to the end of this age—when Satan no longer has access to God? No one knows for sure. One thing is certain, Satan and his demons lose, Michael is victorious, and Satan is thrown to the earth. There he wages war against the woman's offspring, Israel, and those who follow the teachings of Jesus.

But notice who is in control: God. In the meantime, God's people have an enemy who is real and alive. That enemy is powerful, more powerful than you or I. But we are given a strategy to defeat him. "*And they have conquered him by the blood of the Lamb and by the word of their testimony, for they loved not their lives even unto death*" (12:11). The Bible calls us to know Jesus by faith, honor Christ the Lord as holy, and always be ready to give our testimony (1 Peter 3:15).

What is our testimony? It is the story of what Jesus has done in our lives—how he has changed who we are, how we think, and how we respond to life. We all have a testimony, and it is powerful. No one can argue with our testimony; it is ours. People can argue about doctrine and the interpretation of Scripture, but they cannot argue with individual testimony.

> "Satan is defeated. Jesus won the battle on the cross. The resurrection of Jesus was God's stamp of approval of Satan's demise. But Satan still has power. Ephesians 6 speaks of the war that is being waged. "*For we do not wrestle against flesh and blood, but against the rulers, against the authorities, against the cosmic powers over this present darkness, against the spiritual forces of evil in the heavenly places*" (Ephesians 6:12).

And we are to stand firm: "*Therefore take up the whole armor of God, that you may be able to withstand in the evil day, and having done all, to stand firm*" (Ephesians 6:13). The battle is the Lord's, and only Jesus can overcome Satan. But we can stand firm, knowing that the work of the cross never fails. We can trust in the power of the cross, the blood of Jesus, and the victory of Christ. We can be ready with the testimony of our faith.

Why does God go to such lengths to rescue his people? Because we have an enemy who is powerful and hell-bent on destroying all that belongs to God. But Jesus has overcome the foe. "*I have said these things to you, that in me you may have peace. In the world you will have tribulation. But take heart; I have overcome the world*" (John 16:33).

THE LINE IN THE SAND

REVELATION 13

Just when you think things couldn't get worse, they do. Remember, Revelation may be an allegory about our lives on earth, or it can be a reality of things to come.

In every chapter of Revelation, God is in control. But at the beginning of chapter 13, God allows Satan to unleash another character, called "*a beast.*" This creature is from the sea. In first-century times, the sea was thought to be a place of darkness, unpredictability, and evil. The sea often symbolized the pagan nations, so it is interesting that this beast comes from the sea.

Again, this beast may be symbolic. It mimics the four beasts described in Daniel that represented four empires (Daniel 7:23–26). This beast has ten horns, seven heads, and ten crowns. This is a picture of the Antichrist, who will have great power given to him by Satan. He also desires to be king and worshipped by all people. The ten crowns symbolize his kingship over ten nations. This character will have the ferocity of a lion, like ancient Babylon; the crushing power of a bear, like the Medo-Persian empire; and the swiftness of a leopard, like ancient Greece. These ancient empires oppressed the Jewish people and were identified in Daniel's prophecy. The last beast in Daniel is more terrifying than all the rest and bears a striking resemblance to the beast in Revelation. There will come a time when that beast will rule the world and all people on earth will worship him, "*everyone whose name has not been written before the foundation of the world in the book of life of the Lamb who was slain*" (13:8).

So, we have the dragon, Satan, and the first beast, the Antichrist. We are now introduced to a third character, who came from the earth. He had two horns like a lamb but spoke like a dragon. This creature is a fake lamb of God, a counterfeit, a false prophet to demand that all people worship the Antichrist.

Is this possible? Can Satan delude the people so convincingly? He already does. He doesn't wear a red dragon costume with multiple heads; he masquerades as an angel of light (2 Corinthians 11:14). The Antichrist will be appealing, and he will receive a fatal wound. But he will live, and people will flock to him. Today, Satanic worship is gaining ground, but in the end times, it will reach a new height. And the prophet or second beast that resembles a lamb will somehow delude the Hebrew people. Peace will reign on the earth because the beast will ensure that any opposition to him is destroyed. To buy or sell goods, one must take the mark of the beast. To remain faithful to Jesus will involve total commitment. We see this in some countries today, where Christians are denied social rights because of their faith.

The persecution is dreadful. How do those who are faithful to Jesus survive? How can they conquer such a potent threat? Each chapter provides some clues.

The first clue was in Revelation 12:11, saying that the believers "*conquered him [the accuser] by the blood of the Lamb and by the word of their testimony, for they loved not their lives even unto death.*" First and foremost, the blood of Jesus assures us of victory over Satan. And the word of our testimony conquers the enemy's accusations. The testimony of what God has done in your life is powerful. No one can argue with it; no one can denounce it. It is your story, and Satan is powerless over it. We must be ever-ready to share the "*reason for the hope*" that is in us (Hebrews 3:15). We must love Jesus more than our own lives.

Believers can take heart, knowing that this persecution is only for a season—at the most seven years, but more like three and a half years—until God allows the unholy trinity of Satan, the Antichrist, and the false prophet to have full reign. He does this so that the fullness of evil will be shown for what it is. The delusions will evaporate.

As some theologians believe, the Antichrist will set himself up in Jerusalem, in the rebuilt temple. All will seem well until after three and a half years (mid-tribulation). The Antichrist will demand worship and allegiance to himself and the dragon. This is called the abomination that causes desolation.

More than two thousand years ago, Satan tempted Jesus in the desert. One of his temptations was to offer Jesus all the world's kingdoms if he would just bow down to Satan. Jesus refused (Matthew 4:8–10). In Revelation 13, the Antichrist tries to grasp this worldwide power.

At this point, a line is drawn in the sand. Every person must take one side or the other. There is no in-between. Each person must make a choice: the real Lamb that was slain on a hill in Jerusalem or the fake lamb that speaks like the devil. The Jesus who offers peace and grace, or the Antichrist who offers domination and blasphemies of God. The real Jesus wants your worship, your love, and your thankfulness. But the Antichrist wants your worship, and he will kill you if you don't give it to him.

God goes to great lengths to save those who are being deceived. He knows the wiles of Satan, and he knows our weakness. But the power of the risen Christ gives us the power of the Holy Spirit—for patient endurance and faithfulness during times of persecution and suffering (hat we are susceptible if we don't use patient endurance and faithfulness during times of persecution and questioning (Romans 5:3–5; James 1:2).

Again, we ask ourselves: how can God's people have endurance and faith (13:10)? The answer is in the next two chapters.

WEEK
5

A BATTLE FOR SOULS, A CHOICE TO BE MADE

DAY 21

PATIENT ENDURANCE

REVELATION 14 AND 15

Again, we ask ourselves, how can God's people endure? John returns to the sealed multitude of 144,000 that we read about in chapter 7 and expands on who they are. These believers are sold out to Jesus, and they follow the Lamb wherever he goes. They are sexually pure, spiritually pure, truthful, blameless, and devoted to Jesus. They are "redeemed from mankind as firstfruits for God and the Lamb" (14:4).

The Bible is full of songs—from entire books of songs, like the Psalms, the Song of Solomon, and Lamentations; and individual songs from Moses, Miriam, David, Deborah, and more. Even the prayers of Mary and Hannah are often considered songs. But the first named song in the Bible appears in Exodus 15, a song of Moses after the ancient Israelites had crossed the Red Sea and Pharaoh's army had been destroyed by God. The last song in the Bible is also called the song of Moses, sung by those redeemed from the clutches of Satan, the Antichrist, and the false prophet:

"And they sing the song of Moses, the servant of God, and the song of the Lamb, saying,
'Great and amazing are your deeds,
O Lord God the Almighty!
Just and true are your ways,
O King of the nations!
Who will not fear, O Lord,
and glorify your name?
For you alone are holy.
All nations will come
and worship you,
for your righteous acts have been revealed.'" (15:3–4)

By this time, an angel proclaims the eternal Gospel to the entire world. As you may recall, Jesus said this is one of the prerequisites for His return (Mark 13).

Another angel warns that to take the mark of the beast is irrevocable. Those who wear it "will drink the wine of God's wrath, poured full strength into the cup of his anger" (14:10).

Is this the same cup that Jesus asked to be taken from him in the garden of Gethsemane? The prospect of his drinking that cup was too great. But Jesus did drink it. He drank the full strength of the cup of God's wrath for those who believe. Those who don't believe will drink the cup of wrath themselves. This is the last warning.

John's prophecy assures the early Christians of the seven churches that Babylon has fallen. Babylon represents the ancient kingdoms of riches, oppression, and pagan worship. In other words, all the enemies of God's people. If the Jewish occupants of the Nazi concentration camps had known that the Allies would win and they would be liberated within a matter of months, would they have been encouraged? Revelation 14 and 15 share the good news of Christ's eternal victory, so believers don't lose heart as we encounter life's difficulties.

At this point, we see two mighty angels, each with a harvesting sickle. Jesus spoke of this reaping in Matthew 13:40–43. The timeclock of Revelation is now ticking. "*Then I saw another sign in heaven, great and amazing, seven angels with seven plagues, which are the last, for with them the wrath of God is finished*" (15:1). God's people who overcame the dragon and the beast are victorious. Satan's ploys to take down God's people with persecution to death backfires—because, with the believers' martyrdom, Satan becomes the elevator boy that delivers God's people to the heavenly realms. Satan thought he could outmaneuver God, but that is impossible. He couldn't kill the baby Jesus; God intervened in a dream (Matthew 2:12–16). Satan couldn't capture the 144,000 that were sold out to God, and they were given a new song of redemption that only they knew. Satan couldn't put his mark on God's people or deceive them, because they overcame him by the blood of the Lamb and the word of their testimony. Those who know Jesus will suffer, but they suffer with victory in their hearts.

Now the temple of God is off-limits. "*The sanctuary was filled with smoke from the glory of God and from his power, and no one could enter the sanctuary until the seven plagues of the seven angels were finished*" (15:8). The bowl judgments are about to begin. The sides are chosen, and their eternity is set.

As we study these difficult passages in Revelation, we often wonder: How do these prophecies affect our lives? Will the earth keep spinning forever with no real change? We live in a world with evil: bombs in packages, shootings in schools, posturing in politics, and failures in integrity. But we have the victory. Satan has been defeated eternally, and we can deny his power practically as we trust in the blood of the Lamb. We can also take courage in Christ's victory as we share our testimony. How are you doing at that? Is your faith evident to those in the world around you?

"*Here is a call for the endurance and faith of the saints*" (13:10). Are you willing to be as "sold out" to Jesus as those 144,000? Their lives reflect their complete faith. Do ours? Do our prayers reflect our faith and complete confidence in God?

"IT IS DONE!"

REVELATION 16

As we studied the apostate church, we have seen the evil that permeates our world and attempts to take down the church. This is why Jesus came and died. Our sin is the reason for the cross. As we see the evil of the end times, we need to remember the evil done to Jesus. On our behalf, he received foul treatment from the temple guards, insults from the religious leaders, and scourging on the cross. Jesus took the cup of the wrath of God for us. He faced the powerful evil that set itself against God and his people. Jesus saved us from our sins, and he will return to judge the world.

At this point in Revelation, God is moving to establish his kingdom on earth as it is in heaven. In chapter 12, we met a woman who seemed to represent Israel. She was being pursued by the devil (dragon) but was miraculously saved by God. After that, the dragon made war against her children and those who hold to the testimony of Jesus. After meeting the Antichrist and the false prophet, we get a sense that a line is drawn in the sand. Every person must choose either the kingdom of God or the kingdom of Satan. There is no in-between.

We have seen the seven seal judgments, then the seven trumpet judgments, which had limits. Only one-third of earth, man, and beast were destroyed by God. But now, those days of waiting for the wayward to repent are over. Chapter 15 is the announcement of the final seven judgments, called the bowl judgments. The seventh trumpet ends the woe judgments and releases the bowl judgments (see Day 16, Revelation 8).

These final judgments are horrendous. Notice that they resemble the plagues against Egypt (Exodus 7–13). First, the *"painful sores"* in Revelation 16:2 are like the boils in the sixth plague of punishment in ancient Egypt (Exodus 9:8–12).

In the second trumpet judgment, we saw the sea turned to blood—but then, only one-third of the creatures died (8:8). When Moses turned the Nile to blood, everything died, and the people could not drink the water (Exodus 7:14–25). Here in Revelation 16:3, all the water is contaminated as a sign of judgment:

> *"And I heard the angel in charge of the waters say,*
>
> *'Just are you, O Holy One, who is and who was,*
>
> *for you brought these judgments.*
>
> *For they have shed the blood of saints and prophets,*
>
> *and you have given them blood to drink.*
>
> *It is what they deserve!'"* (16:5–6)

In the fourth bowl judgment, the sun becomes the enemy of man and scorches all mankind. Notice that this phenomenon could only come from the hand of God, who rules creation. Note the reaction of the people: *"They were scorched by the fierce heat, and they cursed the name of God who had power over these plagues. They did not repent and give him glory"* (16:9).

Next, *"The fifth angel poured out his bowl on the throne of the beast, and its kingdom was plunged into darkness. People gnawed their tongues in anguish"* (16:10). Again, we saw this in ancient Egypt. During the ninth plague, the Egyptians were plunged into total darkness—but the land of Goshen, where the Hebrews lived, had light (Exodus 10:21–29). Jesus spoke of this fate for unbelievers, who *"will be thrown into the outer darkness. In that place there will be weeping and gnashing of teeth"* (Matthew 8:12). This is a preview of hell, yet the people refused to repent.

The sixth bowl is the beginning of the end. The Euphrates River was a natural boundary between eastern and western countries. In ancient times, the Euphrates River was 1,800 miles long and 300–1,200 yards wide. To dry up this river meant that the armies of the east could easily march on the Holy Land and Europe in the west.

> "And I saw, coming out of the mouth of the dragon and out of the mouth of the beast and out of the mouth of the false prophet, three unclean spirits like frogs. For they are demonic spirits, performing signs, who go abroad to the kings of the whole world, to assemble them for battle on the great day of God the Almighty.... And they assembled them at the place that in Hebrew is called Armageddon" (16:13–14, 16).

This assembly is gathering for the final battle of good versus evil. Armageddon means hill or mountain of Megiddo. Megiddo is located south of present-day Haifa in the Esdraelon plain. This location has been the place of many ancient battles, and recently as a battle in World War II. It is here that Napoleon said, "Here indeed, all the armies of the earth may gather for battle."

Frogs like evil spirits unleash from the mouths of the dragon, the beast, and the false prophet—and they go throughout the world to win over and dominate the kings of the earth. The Jews saw frogs as unclean, nasty animals. However, ancient Egypt worshipped frogs and considered them a source of creation and fertility.

Jesus inserts a warning in the middle of the bowl judgments, *"Behold, I am coming like a thief! Blessed is the one who stays awake, keeping his garments on, that he may not go about naked and be seen exposed!"* (16:15). This is reminiscent of Galatians 3:27, *"For as many of you as were baptized into Christ have put on* [are clothed in] *Christ."* Many of the parables of Jesus are about staying vigilant, staying awake, so as not to miss the coming of the Lord (Matthew 24:42; Mark 13:35; Luke 21:36). Believers are clothed with the righteousness of Christ (2 Corinthians 5:4, Revelation 3:5).

The final bowl is an earthquake that divides the great city into three parts. What city? Most likely Jerusalem. This coincides with the prophecy in Zechariah 14, where Jesus will stand on the Mount of Olives, which will split in two, providing a way to freedom for God's people in the end times.

Throughout this chapter, God is pouring out supernatural wrath, and the people's hearts are so hard that they refuse to come to the Lord and repent. Instead, they curse God (16:21). Then *"the seventh angel poured out his bowl into the air, and a loud voice came out of the temple, from the throne, saying, 'It is done!'"* (16:17).

God declares, "Time is up!" All those who come to the Lord have come. Like the door to Noah's ark, the time is closed, and judgment is at hand. Babylon the Great will endure the cup filled with the fury of God's wrath (16:20).

The last time we read the words *"It is done"* was from Jesus on the cross (John 19:30). His work was completed, and he opened the door to salvation from sin and death. Now God says, *"It is done."* His work of establishing his son's kingdom on earth as it is in heaven is happening. *"The kingdom of the world has become the kingdom of our Lord and of his Christ, and he shall reign forever and ever"* (11:15).

DAY 23

THE GREAT WHORE

REVELATION 17 AND 18

Who is Babylon the Great, and why does it deserve such wrath? Chapters 17 and 18 answer that question.

The city of Babylon dates back to the time of Genesis. The Tower of Babel, where the people wanted to make a name for themselves, was its nucleus. The city was later established by Nimrod, who was called the great hunter of human souls. Fast-forward many years, and Babylon at the time of Daniel was the most powerful and wealthiest empire on earth. Their king invaded Judah in 587 BC and took captive all the Jews, leaving only a remnant in the Holy Land. Over time, Babylon has been a symbol of pagan idolatry and spiritual adultery against the true God. In chapter 17, John gives us a word picture of what Babylon is like.

In chapter 12, we saw a woman who symbolizes Israel or Mary. She is crowned with twelve stars and clothed with the sun and the moon under her feet. She is attacked by the dragon Satan, who wants to kill her child, Jesus—but God saves her and her Son (12:5–6). Therefore, the dragon makes war against her offspring, those who hold to the teachings of Jesus. The woman in chapter 12 represents purity and honor, but the woman in chapter 17 represents filth, prostitution, intoxication, and adultery. The woman dressed in the sun (12:1) is the antithesis of the woman dressed in scarlet and purple, with her glittering stones, gold, and pearls. This wicked woman even holds a golden cup full of abominations and impurities (17:4). The woman in chapter 12 stands on a cloud, but the woman in chapter 17 sits on a red beast with ten horns and seven heads—the Antichrist, given power by Satan (13:1–2). The prostitute, who rides the beast, represents the world's false religions. At the end times, this false faith will be global, enticing, and prosperous. This enemy of Jesus will wield miraculous powers that can deceive.

Two women: one following Jesus and the other following Satan. The prostitute is glamorous, bejeweled, sensual, and attractive to those who do not know Jesus. She is the counterfeit of the pure and righteous woman. All people are offspring of one or the other.

The beast with seven heads is symbolic of seven hills. Some believe these are the seven hills where Rome sits, and it may play an important negative role at the end times. And the seven heads are the seven kings under the power of the Beast. The seven heads also mirror the dragon, the beast's master and authority (13:3–4).

The events that follow in Revelation 17:8–18 have many different interpretations. Note the description in these two verses: "*they are also seven kings, five of whom have fallen, one is, the other has not yet come, and when he does come he must remain only a little while. As for the beast that was and is not, it is an eighth but it belongs to the seven, and it goes to destruction*" (17:10–11).

Throughout the years, theologians have tried to mark the empires. A common interpretation names Babylon, Assyria, Egypt, Persia, and Greece (the five empires that had fallen at the time of John's writing). These are the first five kings.

Rome is the that existed at John's writings, the sixth king.

Then one "*who has not yet come,*" but will remain a little while, then the beast, the seventh and eighth kings (17:11).

Then John goes back to the ten horns of the beast. "*And the ten horns that you saw are ten kings who have not yet received royal power, but they are to receive authority as kings for one hour, together with the beast*" (17:12). Horns symbolize power. After the beast has come to power, ten kings again controlled by Satan and the Antichrist will emerge as a confederation. They will give their power to the beast and have one purpose, to make war against the Lamb and his followers. These kings seem to represent a worldwide economic consortium, and the woman represents the false religion. At a point in time, the ten kings led by the beast will turn against the false religious leaders represented by the woman and destroy them. Evidently, having only economic power is not enough; they also want religious power. Some theologians believe this false worldwide religion will be overcome at the mid-point of the tribulation. Evil will destroy itself from within.

Is Babylon a real city? Or is it the apostate church that looks like a church, smells like a church, talks like a church, but is not a true church of Jesus Christ? Is Rome to be a part of the story at the end times? With God's people raptured, does Rome come to the front—not as a true church, but a fake one? Does Islam play a role in this drama? Or is this all symbolism? Is it written to remind us to follow Jesus as the way, the truth, the light, and the life—while we stand firm against the dark forces surrounding us that strive to waylay our faith?

The wrath of God is massive for the prostitute of Babylon the Great. From the garden of Eden, Satan has used manipulation and lies to lead people away from the true God.

"*This calls for a mind with wisdom*" for Christians (17:9). James says, "*If any of you lacks wisdom, let him ask God, who gives generously to all without reproach, and it will be given him*" (James 1:5). The bottom line is that there have been and will be governments who do not hold to the teachings of Jesus. They form a bond with evil. But Christians do not have to fear—we can trust, be alert, and seek wisdom from God. He will answer.

....

....

....

....

....

....

....

....

....

....

....

....

....

....

....

....

....

FINALLY, JUDGMENT

REVELATION 18

Chapter 18 starts with a mighty angel announcing, *"Fallen, fallen is Babylon the great!"* (18:2). Why? Chapter 18 gives three reasons:

1. This fake religion is demonic (18:2). Demonic forces can get a foothold in the church, and we need to be vigilant against false teaching that compromises the truth of the Gospel. *Babylon has fallen, and "She has become a dwelling place for demons, a haunt for every unclean spirit, a haunt for every unclean bird, a haunt for every unclean and detestable beast"* (18:2). These unclean animals represent defilement (Isaiah 13:21; 34:14; Jeremiah 50–51). Tolerance for wrong beliefs can enter through the back door and corrupt the church from within.

2. With demonic influence comes adultery, both physical and ideological (18:3). Babylon spread her corruption like a plague. Unfaithfulness was her hallmark, compared to the faithfulness that characterizes God. She enticed nations with her wealth and luxuries. To worship this false religion meant material affluence.

3. *In arrogance, pride, and self-indulgence, she declares, "I sit as a queen, I am no widow, and mourning I shall never see" (18:7).* Her sinful attributes show her corruption, and Scripture is clear: *"This calls for a mind with wisdom"* (17:9).

The rest of chapter 18 shows two different reactions to the fall of Babylon. The first reaction is from those who have grown rich off Babylon's religious corruption. Notice that they stand far off and seem most distraught over their loss of income. The materials they will lose are listed in Revelation 18:11–13—and they are all luxury items. Most disturbing in the list is the last one, *"human souls."* This could be the sex slave market, or a future captivity that erupts when God's hand allows evil to have its full course. The wealthy merchants are appalled that so great and powerful an institution could be destroyed in one hour.

"And they threw dust on their heads as they wept and mourned, crying out, 'Alas, alas, for the great city where all who had ships at sea grew rich by her wealth! For in a single hour she has been laid waste'" (18:19).

When these last judgments occur, it will be like childbirth. Labor pains begin slowly, but they get more intense and rapid as the birth draws near. This will be the case in the birthing of God's kingdom on earth. But even at this point in the judgment, God the Father shows mercy.

"Then I heard another voice from heaven saying, 'Come out of her, my people, lest you take part in her sins, lest you share in her plagues; for her sins are heaped high as heaven, and God has remembered her iniquities'" (18:4–5). Wake up! Don't go down into the depths with this fake religion. Be smart; use wisdom. Read the Word, know what it says. Pray. Ask God to lead you in the paths of righteousness.

The second reaction to this judgment comes in chapter 19—rejoicing! God's people see the end of the evil institutions, and the martyrs are avenged.

At this point in the story, I'm ready to sing the Hallelujah Chorus! But we will save that for next week. Instead, the words of these chapters remind me of the power of the cross. Satan is powerful, but the blood of the Lamb has won! We resist the enemy with the word of our testimony and the willingness to give our lives for him.

The beast is powerful and wants all people to worship him. He supports a false religion that on the outside may seem OK—but if you look deeper, you see that it does not hold to sound doctrine, "*in accordance with the gospel of the glory of the blessed God*" (1 Timothy 1:11). That's why we study the Word. That's why we contend for the faith (Jude 3). That is why chapter 1 told us that those who read this book and take it to heart are blessed. They will be able to see the signs of the end times, they will be able to identify compromise, and they will be able to shed the light of God's Word to others. The false prophet is powerful, too, and he will push people to worship the beast. But they will all come to an end.

Jesus is the true Lamb, and God is in control. Next week, his glory is proclaimed. It's going to be loud!

HALLELUJAH, HE'S HERE

REVELATION 19:1–10

It is time for the Hallelujah Chorus. Revelation 19 is the moment that all God's people have waited for. It is the second coming of Jesus, the most prophesied event in the Bible.

At the first coming of Jesus, only a few knew of his arrival in Bethlehem. He came as a helpless baby, vulnerable and innocent. At his second coming, the entire earth will see his arrival as a mighty, glorious commander who will strike terror in the hearts of men. At his first coming, he came in peace to draw all who would come to the living God. At his second coming, he will arrive ready for battle to judge the world. His first arrival was accompanied by a star, but his second coming will be accompanied by a majestic army of his followers. At his first coming, he was dressed in swaddling clothes. At his second coming, he will be dressed in a robe dipped in blood. At his first coming, he satisfied the wrath of God. At his second coming, he will tread the winepress of the fury of the wrath of God. At his first coming, only a few knew that he was the King of the Jews. At his second coming, all will know that he is King of kings and Lord of lords.

At this point, the apostate church has been destroyed by the Antichrist and his followers. Evil has turned on evil. The followers of Jesus have been tortured and killed for not bowing to the Antichrist. The altar of martyrs that we read about in chapter 6 will be avenged. The ten kings that followed the Antichrist are now poised to meet at Armageddon. But at some point, possibly before that, we read of heaven giving glory to God.

Hallelujah means "Praise the Lord." It is used here for the first time in the New Testament. *"Hallelujah!"* (19:1). The real church, the bride of Christ, steps forward for the wedding of the Lamb. The time of the church age has come to an end, and now the church takes her rightful place alongside her beloved Savior, Jesus.

> "'Hallelujah! For the Lord our God the Almighty reigns. Let us rejoice and exult and give him the glory, for the marriage of the Lamb has come, and his Bride has made herself ready; it was granted her to clothe herself with fine linen, bright and pure'—for the fine linen is the righteous deeds of the saints" (19:6–8).

Notice that the bride has made herself ready. How? By believing in the Lamb of God and living her testimony. The white, clean linen that she wears is a gift from God. The bride is the authentic church, and the angel instructs John to write: "*Blessed are those who are invited to the marriage supper of the Lamb*" (19:9). First-century Jews believed that their bloodline earned them acceptance into the kingdom of God. They thought that they deserved to sit at the table with the patriarchs. But Jesus says that the only qualification now is belief in him.

The Beloved will celebrate a feast for his bride. And who is invited? All who know Jesus. All humanity is offered an opportunity to receive a wedding invitation—but only believers can send in the reply card that they will attend. This is so overwhelming to John that he starts to worship the angelic messenger.

> "Then I fell down at his feet to worship him, but he said to me, 'You must not do that! I am a fellow servant with you and your brothers who hold to the testimony of Jesus. Worship God.' For the testimony of Jesus is the spirit of prophecy" (19:10).

From the beginning of time, the purpose of prophecy is the revelation of Jesus Christ.

WEEK
6

HE IS COMING!
A PROMISE FULFILLED

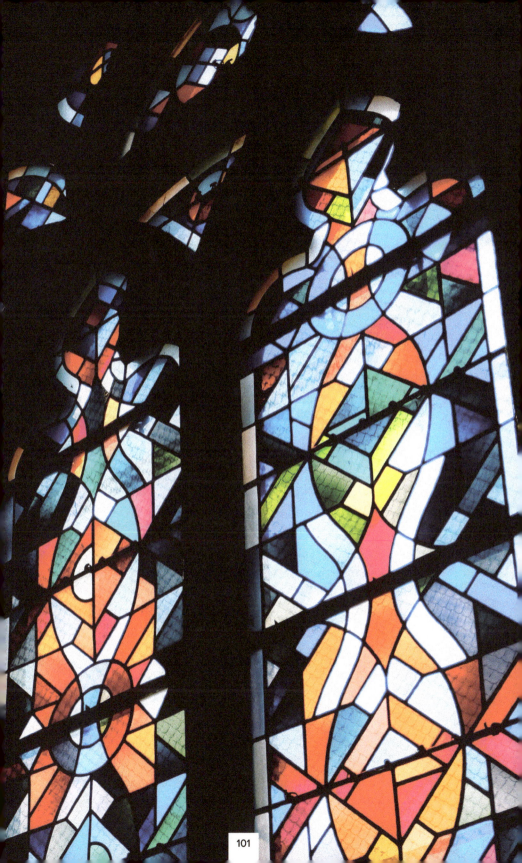

VICTORY IN JESUS!

REVELATION 19:11–19

Full of symbolism, verses 11–19 are my favorites. Heaven opens, and a majestic rider appears:

> "Then I saw heaven opened, and behold, a white horse! The one sitting on it is called Faithful and True, and in righteousness he judges and makes war" (19:11).

The horse is a symbol of a warrior. Before his crucifixion, Jesus entered Jerusalem on a colt, the foal of a donkey (Matthew 21:1–11; Mark 11:1–11; Luke 19:28–40; John 12:12). The donkey was a service beast, chosen to fulfill the prophecy of the humble king: "*Behold, your king is coming to you; righteous and having salvation is he, humble and mounted on a donkey, on a colt, the foal of a donkey*" (Zechariah 9:9). But Jesus knew that he would return as the warrior on the horse, to claim not just the throne of David but his eternal throne.

> "His eyes are like a flame of fire, and on his head are many diadems, and he has a name written that no one knows but himself" (19:12).

His eyes are like blazing fire, judging with penetrating vision. The many crowns show kingship over many nations and could also represent the crowns given to believers as rewards that are placed at the feet of Jesus. His name, written that no one knows but he himself, is part of the mystery of his eternal, Trinitarian kingship.

> "He is clothed in a robe dipped in blood, and the name by which he is called is The Word of God. And the armies of heaven, arrayed in fine linen, white and pure, were following him on white horses" (19:13–14).

He is dressed in a robe dipped in blood—the blood he shed to atone for our sins, the evidence of his completed work on the cross. The armies of heaven, dressed in fine white linen, are the followers of Jesus, washed clean and made pure by his blood.

> "From his mouth comes a sharp sword with which to strike down the nations, and he will rule them with a rod of iron. He will tread the winepress of the fury of the wrath of God the Almighty" (19:15).

Out of his mouth comes a sharp sword to strike down the nations. His word is convicting and can cut through pretense and deception. All nations will be exposed for who they are. He rules the nations with an iron scepter, with his unbendable justice and authority over all nations. The standard of righteousness is God's holiness, not man's morality.

He treads the winepress of the fury of the wrath of God Almighty. Jesus drank the cup of the wrath of God at the cross. Now those who stand against Jesus and God will be punished for their evil acts.

> "On his robe and on his thigh he has a name written, King of kings and Lord of lords" (19:16).

His name is on his robe and thigh, the symbol of strength in a man and where a warrior would keep his sword. His name—King of kings and Lord of lords—shouts to the enemies who he is and what he claims.

Most commentators agree that verses 17–21 speak of the battle between good and evil, in the heavenly realms or on the earth.

> "And I saw the beast and the kings of the earth with their armies gathered to make war against him who was sitting on the horse and against his army" (19:19).

These verses make it clear who wins. The power of the Word of God annihilates a massive army. The birds of the air are invited to the great supper of God—on the bodies of the enemy. There are two feasts: the wedding feast of the Lamb and the gory feast that marks God's victory over his enemies. All people will be present at one feast or the other. In one feast, believers celebrate the marriage of the Lamb; in the other, unbelievers serve as carrion for the birds. The fate of the Antichrist and the false prophet is to be thrown alive into the lake of fire.

God wins, Jesus is victorious, and we are there. But as believers, we experience Christ's victory even now. Life brings trials, and the enemy strives to get us to renounce God during times of suffering. We struggle against our sin, but Christ has the victory! (Romans 7:21–25). When we cling to Jesus, our lives bear eternal fruit and testimony to him (John 15:5–8).

Is this battle real? Will it really happen on earth at Armageddon? Or is it spiritual? Many commentators believe that there will be a change in the world as we know it. But the battle is real, whether on earth or in the heavenlies (Ephesians 6:12). Whose side are you on?

....

....

....

....

....

....

....

....

....

....

....

....

....

....

....

....

....

....

THE MILLENNIAL KINGDOM

REVELATION 20

In chapter 20, it finally happens. Satan is bound and thrown into the Abyss. He is chained and locked inside the exit so that no one can get in and nothing can get out. That is, no one but God.

This chapter is clear that there are two resurrections: the first resurrection involving all who have faith in Jesus Christ. Those who are faithful during the tribulation are raised to life and reign with Jesus. Those who have died before this time (probably you and me) are not resurrected bodily until after the thousand-year reign of Jesus on earth. Does this mean that when I die, I'm not with the Lord Jesus? No, at death, our spirits are immediately with Jesus (Luke 23:43; Hebrews 9:27). But our resurrected bodies—which will bear a similarity to Jesus's resurrected body—will not join us for eternity until after his reign on earth. This is the first resurrection of our bodies. We come to our heavenly home ready for worship, and we don't have to worry about the second death.

What is the second death? All those who refused Jesus come to life and are judged according to what they have done (20:12). No one can stand before the Lord in their own righteousness: "*If you, O LORD, should mark iniquities, O Lord, who could stand?*" (Psalm 130:3). Their deeds cannot make up for their rejection of Jesus. They experience the second death in the lake of fire.

And what about Satan? He and his cohorts are in the Abyss, but after one thousand years, something terrible happens. Satan is released. Who releases Satan? God. Why? Because there is rebellion (again). Gog and Magog are mentioned as supporting Satan in this final rebellion. These two names come from Ezekiel 38 and 39, which predict that the Jews will be living securely in their land when Gog invades them. The Lord God will furiously retaliate and destroy Gog: "*So I will show my greatness and my holiness and make myself known in the eyes of many nations. Then they will know that I am the LORD*" (Ezekiel 38:23).

God's judgment declares his greatness and power. Afterward, Ezekiel promises the restoration of the descendants of Jacob. The Jewish people will be regathered to their land, and God's face will never again be hidden from the Jewish people. Some theologians believe that this Gog (whose land was Magog) was far from the Lord's Holy City of Jerusalem.

This prophecy could mean that, even in the millennial kingdom with Jesus ruling, there will be those who drift far away from him and are used as fodder for Satan's tricks. In the end, the battle will be short, and God himself will destroy the rebels. This is the last we hear of Satan, who will burn in the lake of fire forever.

So, we have seen the seal judgments and the trumpet judgments, all trying to convince those who don't know God to come to him through Jesus. Times are tough, but God's people are secure in the outcome and their final destination. The apostate religion is destroyed along with the evil political system that permeates the world. Jesus arrives in the fullness of his glory. He faces off with the mighty forces of evil and is victorious. This sets in motion a millennial kingdom where Jesus rules with an iron scepter.

Again, mankind rebels with Satan in the lead, and all are destroyed for good. All are judged. Your sins are either on the cross or on you. "*He himself bore our sins in his body on the tree, that we might die to sin and live to righteousness. By his wounds you have been healed*" (1 Peter 2:24).

Those who refuse Jesus are brought back to life to be judged at the great white throne. They are condemned.

So, what do we do with this information? How are we blessed by this book if we can't even understand it?

The book of Revelation affirms that evil exists in this world—and we need to be aware of that. There will be a time when God will judge the people. And God is sovereign today. No matter what is happening in my life, Jesus has won the victory, and he intercedes for me. Satan, the Antichrist, and the false prophet are no match for God the Father, Jesus the Son, and the Holy Spirit.

At times it may look as if Satan is winning, but it is only a skirmish. The final battle is done; it was achieved at the cross. I am safe in the cross. My eternal destiny is secure. I will be with Jesus for eternity.

> "For I know that my Redeemer lives, and at the last he will stand upon the earth. And after my skin has been thus destroyed, yet in my flesh I shall see God, whom I shall see for myself, and my eyes shall behold, and not another. My heart faints within me!" (Job 19:25–27). I yearn for that day, don't you?

CHRIST IN US, THE HOPE OF GLORY

REVELATION 21

This is the moment that Jesus has longed for, the moment he endured the cross for—the moment when he finally can embrace his beloved bride.

Have you ever felt that you were made for something greater than what this earth has to offer? Have you ever felt that there must be something more to life than just living on earth, trudging through life, and dying? Well, you're right. There is something more. The end of the Bible is the bookend to the beginning of the Bible: "*In the beginning, God created the heavens and the earth*" (Genesis 1:1). When God finished his work of creation, he saw that what he made was very good (Genesis 1:31). We might look with longing hearts back to the garden of Eden—the time when Adam and Eve experienced pure innocence, joy, abundance, and communion with God as he walked in the garden in the cool of the evening. We might feel a little resentment with Adam and Eve for falling into sin.

The fellowship with God was broken. But from the beginning, God knew that man would fall. Sin would enter the world, and innocence would be lost. As sinners, we are bruised, broken, dirtied, and maimed by our walk in a world full of uncertainty and evil. But in the book of Revelation, believers are called overcomers (21:7). Through the blood of Jesus, we are called sons of God. We reflect his mercy, power, and glory as we "*shine like the sun in the kingdom*" (Matthew 13:43).

Chapters 21 and 22 describe what the eternal home of believers looks like. These chapters provide the most detail about our permanent dwelling place with God. Ezekiel 47 gives us a similar picture.

Why does God need to create a new heaven and new earth? Because the old world has been tainted and destroyed. In Romans 8, we read that the creation which God saw as good was subject to frustration by the curse at the fall of man.

> "For the creation waits with eager longing for the revealing of the sons of God. For the creation was subjected to futility, not willingly, but because of him who subjected it, in hope that the creation itself will be set free from its bondage to corruption and obtain the freedom of the glory of the children of God" (Romans 8:19–21).

At the end of the age, heaven and earth will be reborn. We are transformed and purified at our spiritual rebirth when we come to faith in Jesus (1 John 3:3). It seems that the heavens and earth will experience a similar transformation. *"But according to his promise we are waiting for new heavens and a new earth in which righteousness dwells"* (2 Peter 3:13).

This new heaven and new earth will be defined in part by what they *don't* have:

No sea. *"The sea was no more"* (21:1). In the first century, the sea represented the unknown, the fearful sea monsters, and the place where the Antichrist emerged. But in the new heavens and new earth, the sea is no longer there. Gone is the fear of the unknown and the fear of the sea's dark depths.

No more death. *"Death shall be no more"* (21:4). Fear of death is a non-issue because we will be in our immortal bodies. *"So is it with the resurrection of the dead. What is sown is perishable; what is raised is imperishable... The first man Adam became a living being; the last Adam became a life-giving spirit.... Just as we have borne the image of the man of dust, we shall also bear the image of the man of heaven.... When the perishable puts on the imperishable, and the mortal puts on immortality, then shall come to pass the saying that is written: 'Death is swallowed up in victory'"* (1 Corinthians 15:42, 47, 49, 54).

No more mourning, crying, or pain. From a baby's first breath, a cry comes forth from its lungs as the first breath painfully expands the lungs. Life has pain. If you live long enough, you will mourn for loved ones who die. From the middle of troubling circumstances, David proclaimed his trust in God: *"You have kept count of my tossings; put my tears in your bottle. Are they not in your book?"* (Psalm 56:8). God sees our tears and counts our troubles. Jesus took on human flesh and he understands our human temptations (Hebrews 4:15). But in the new heavens and new earth, all our pain is gone.

No more sin. In his letter to the Corinthians, Paul lists the unrighteous that will not inherit the kingdom of God: *"neither the sexually immoral, nor idolaters, nor adulterers, nor men who practice homosexuality, nor thieves, nor the greedy, nor drunkards, nor revilers, nor swindlers will inherit the kingdom of God."* But then he reminds us, *"such were some of you. But you were washed, you were sanctified, you were justified in the name of the Lord Jesus Christ and by the Spirit of our God"* (1 Corinthians 6:10–11). The blood of the Lamb has atoned for our sins. But all those who do not repent will be condemned to the fiery lake of burning sulfur. The second death does not affect God's people whose names are written in the Lamb's book of life.

No temple. God and the Lamb are its temple. Worship goes on 24/7, and we are a part of the glory of the heavenly host.

No sun or moon. God's glory gives light and the Lamb is the lamp.

No night. Light now permanently conquers the darkness.

No curse. The curse that mankind inherited from Adam is now over.

When John saw the image of the Holy City, the New Jerusalem, he compared it to the beauty of a bride dressed for her wedding day.

What is different about this new city?

God resides there. No longer is there fear of seeing the face of God and dying (Exodus 33:20). The Holy God comes near to wipe every tear from the eyes of his children. He is tender and close, like a father with his child or a husband with his wife.

In verse 5, God speaks from the throne for the first time. "*And he who was seated on the throne said, 'Behold, I am making all things new.' Also he said, 'Write this down, for these words are trustworthy and true.'*" In other words, you can count on it. His words are true.

Then God says, "*It is done*" (21:6). Pastor and theologian Michael Wilcock commented on this verse: "In Eden, the work of creation was finished (Genesis 2:1–2); at Calvary, the work of redemption was finished (John 19:30); in paradise the voice of God will finally say, concerning the whole of his work, 'It is done.'"[1]

He then goes back to how he first identified himself in chapter 1 of Revelation: the Alpha and Omega, the beginning and the end. The gift of the water of life is for anyone who is thirsty—thirsty for God, thirsty for the Savior. Jesus called sinners to find their satisfaction in him: "*If anyone thirsts, let him come to me and drink. Whoever believes in me, as the Scripture has said, 'Out of his heart will flow rivers of living water'*" (John 7:37–38).

Salvation is a gift; we don't have to pay for it because it has already been purchased at the cross.

---

1   Michael Wilcock, *The Message of Revelation*, vol. 52 of *The Bible Speaks Today,* ed. John Stott (Downers Grove, IL: InterVarsity Press, 1975).

> "The one who conquers will have this heritage, and I will be his God and he will be my son" (21:7). This promise takes us back to the study of the seven churches. Each one had overcomers who were rewarded by the Lord Jesus. "For everyone who has been born of God overcomes the world. And this is the victory that has overcome the world—our faith. Who is it that overcomes the world except the one who believes that Jesus is the Son of God?" (1 John 5:4–5).

It all comes back to Jesus. When Jesus taught his disciples how to pray, he began with "*Our Father*" (Matthew 6:9). That inclusive pronoun *our* was monumental for first-century Jews. Yahweh was so holy they could not even say his name or be in his presence for fear of death (Deuteronomy 28:58). But in these two simple words, Jesus calls him "*Abba*," Daddy (Mark 14:36; Romans 8:14; Galatians 4:6). He is our Father, too. We are adopted into his home, dwell in his presence, and commune with him as only his children can.

When you think of man, why does God put up with us (Psalm 8)? We are the only thing in creation that is like him, made in his image. He sent his Son in the likeness of sinful man to save us from our sins so that we can have eternal communion with him (Hebrews 2:5–18). Our holiness is assured by the sacrifice of Jesus.

GLORY EMBRACED

REVELATION 21:9–27

Next, the angel says to John, "*Come, I will show you the Bride, the wife of the Lamb*" (21:9). He is describing the City of God, the New Jerusalem. The bride has become the wife, and the marriage has been consummated. God's people are complete in every detail and ready to reign and dwell with him eternally.

The city is described in verses 10–21: "*Coming down out of heaven from God,*" the city is God's gift. Glory emanates from it, and it glows with radiant beauty like a crystal-clear jasper jewel. The city is surrounded by great high walls and twelve pearl gates that never close and have the names of the twelve tribes of Israel. Jesus said in John 4:22 that "*salvation is from the Jews.*" Jesus was the one through whom the entire world would be blessed, as promised to Abraham (Genesis 12:1–3). The gates face all directions so that all can enter.

Each gate is made of a single pearl—an architectural and natural marvel. A pearl is created through the process of pain. When a grain of sand gets embedded into an oyster, the oyster repeatedly covers the painful area with luster. The result is a pearl. This speaks of the cross—the pain of the cross produced a glorious pearl of salvation. Jesus said that "*the kingdom of heaven is like a merchant in search of fine pearls, who, on finding one pearl of great value, went and sold all that he had and bought it*" (Matthew 13:45–46).

The foundation is named for the twelve apostles, and each foundation is a glorious gem. The Gospel message is the undergirding, the support of this great and holy city. Twelve is the number of government and completion. Isaiah prophesied this:

"For to us a child is born, to us a son is given; and the government shall be upon his shoulder, and his name shall be called Wonderful Counselor, Mighty God, Everlasting Father, Prince of Peace. Of the increase of his government and of peace there will be no end, on the throne of David and over his kingdom, to establish it and to uphold it with justice and with righteousness from this time forth and forevermore. The zeal of the LORD of hosts will do this" (Isaiah 9:6–7).

The street is of pure gold, which speaks of deity and glory. I love the fact that there is no need for the moon or sun. The radiance of God the Father illuminates as no sun or moon can. And somehow, Jesus is the lamp through which the glory shines. Notice that Jesus is called the Lamb. Not Jesus the King or Jesus the High Priest or Jesus the Shepherd. He is the sacrificed Lamb of God, and he opened the way for total communion with God the Father. It is God's light that shines through Jesus and Jesus's light that shines through us. This New Jerusalem will be the centerpiece of all nations. The gates are open, but only those whose sins are washed clean by the blood of the Lamb Jesus can dwell there.

This has all been God's plan from the beginning. What a God we worship! What a Father we love!

"See what kind of love the Father has given to us, that we should be called children of God!" (1 John 3:1).

....

....

....

....

....

....

....

....

....

....

COME!

REVELATION 22

The crystal-clear river of the water of life flows from the throne of God and the Lamb. Notice how this place is teeming with life and glory. Even the tree of life that we saw in the garden of Eden grows in this glorious place. Adam and Eve were banished from this tree so that they could not grasp eternal life while they were still unredeemed. But now, everyone in the heavenly city has access to the leaves that heal nations.

In this new creation, kings of the earth that once gathered against the Lamb are coming to give glory to the Lamb. Are they the same kings? Probably not, but the meaning is that God's glory will be so manifest that all will want to come. All glory and honor will be placed where it belongs, in God's dwelling. To have access to the tree of life, one must wash their robes in the blood of the Lamb.

> "No longer will there be anything accursed, but the throne of God and of the Lamb will be in it, and his servants will worship him. They will see his face, and his name will be on their foreheads. And night will be no more. They will need no light of lamp or sun, for the Lord God will be their light, and they will reign forever and ever" (22:3–5).

We serve God and the Lamb. Our eternal lives will be full of remarkable discovery and everlasting joy. We will be active, doing things. Heaven will not be boring.

Verses 6–21 are the epilogue. Repeated again and again is the phrase, *"I am coming soon."* Jesus also attaches two titles to himself. The first is the Root the Offspring of David—a Messianic title that proves God's covenant with King David, that his throne would be established forever.

The second is the bright Morning Star. To clear up any confusion, Satan is referred to as a morning star in which the Hebrew word means "shining one." But Jesus names himself THE Morning Star, the light that breaks through the night sky and ushers in the morning sun. Jesus breaks through the darkness of evil and ushers in salvation. Satan tried to be the counterfeit star and failed.

Is Jesus coming soon? By human accounting, "soon" does not include more than two thousand years. But aren't we all just a breath away from his second coming, to take us home to our citizenship in heaven? Yes. This is one of the most important messages of Revelation. Don't wait! Move now. Get right with God. Believe in Jesus. Come to terms with your limits as a human. Don't put off embracing Jesus as your Lord and Savior. Bow to his authority and accept his ways as your ways. Die to self; don't let the flesh rule you. Believe in Jesus!

A time will come when it is too late. What we believe on earth and do on earth has eternal ramifications. This book should propel us to pray for those who do not believe in God. It should spawn a new passion to proclaim Jesus whenever we are given an opportunity. It should encourage you to "*let your light shine before others, so that they may see your good works and give glory to your Father who is in heaven*" (Matthew 5:16).

The invitation that rings out to the universe is, "*The Spirit and the Bride say, 'Come!' And let him who hears say, 'Come!' Whoever is thirsty, let him come; and whoever wishes, let him take the free gift of the water of life*" (22:17). Notice that the bride invites along with the Spirit. Through the power of the Holy Spirit, we can discern when it is time to proclaim the Gospel so that others can hear it.

For the believer, the message of the Gospel brings security, joy, and peace. We are loved by God the Father as he loves his Son. Jesus in his High Priestly Prayer said it best:

> "*I do not ask for these only, but also for those who will believe in me through their word, that they may all be one, just as you, Father, are in me, and I in you, that they also may be in us, so that the world may believe that you have sent me. The glory that you have given me I have given to them, that they may be one even as we are one, I in them and you in me, that they may become perfectly one, so that the world may know that you sent me and loved them even as you loved me. Father, I desire that they also, whom you have given me, may be with me where I am, to see my glory that you have given me because you loved me before the foundation of the world*" (John 17:20–24).

Do you feel loved? You should. The Creator of the universe gave his beloved Son so that you would have life with him for eternity. Praise God, who has "*made known how great among the Gentiles are the riches of the glory of this mystery, which is **Christ in you, the hope of glory***" (Colossians 1:27).

STUDY GUIDE

Using This Study

HOW TO GET THE MOST OUT OF THIS STUDY

As with any individual or small group study of God's Word, you largely reap what you sow. You get out of it what you put into it. Additionally, some guidelines can help you get the most from your efforts. Here are some suggestions to review before you get started.

1.   Review the Table of Contents. The section entitled "Small Group Leader Helps" lays out best practices for how to host and facilitate a healthy small group and avoid common mistakes. It's a great idea to review this material before having your first meeting.

2.   This book is a tool for facilitation. Adapt it to the needs of your group. If a line of discussion leads to green pastures outside the scope of the book, enjoy the leading of the Good Shepherd. Feel free to ask, or allow other members to ask insightful questions as the Holy Spirit leads.

3.   There is a lot of material here. You do not have to ask every question in your group discussion. Feel free to skip questions as needed and linger over the ones where there is authentic conversation.

4.   Enjoy the experience. Christian community should be characterized by joy and love. Encourage yourself and the group members to bear such fruit. Pray before each session—ask God to minister to you, the facilitator, and every group member by name. Pray for the discussion, the fellowship, and the personal application.

5.   Read the "Outline of Each Session" on the following pages so you understand the flow of the session and how the study works.

OUTLINE OF EACH SESSION

OPENING AND CLOSING PRAYER

Begin and end each session with prayer. Invite God into the midst of your conversation. Use the prayers provided or offer one of your own. The prayers provided could be offered by a member of the group or you could all say them together. Close your group with an offer to pray with one another. There is a prayer journal on page 152 where you can keep track of prayer requests and God's answers to your prayers.

KEY VERSE

Each session begins with a key verse. This verse is a key to understanding the entire week's theme. You may want to memorize these verses. By committing portions of God's Word to long-term memory, you can always refer to them, even when you don't have a Bible with you.

OPENING QUESTIONS

As you gather, a couple of questions are offered to help engage the topic and theme of the selected Scripture for the lesson. They also help build mutual trust with one another. Use the opening questions as an opportunity to reconnect each week and re-engage in the discussion.

SCRIPTURE QUESTIONS

PAYING ATTENTION TO THE TEXT AND MAKING OBSERVATIONS
The Scripture readings and video teachings serve as a unit to help you focus on the key ideas of the lesson, uncovering and developing God's promises in the assigned Scripture.

The initial questions under this section help group members make observations and interpret the text. Use as many or as few of these questions as proves helpful.

The video segment will provide teaching on the passage and direction for the session, serving as a launchpad for your discussion. You can watch this video ahead of the meeting as individuals, or if possible, watch it as a group. If you are hosting this group as an online group and are experiencing diminished quality, you may need to encourage members to take time to watch the video on their own rather than try to play it through your online meeting platform.

The "Video Notes" section offers summaries of key points or big concepts from the video teaching. You may want to ask the group a simple question after the video, something like: "What resonated with you from that video teaching?"

The notes section provides space to take notes as you watch the video or hear inspirational thoughts from the Lord or members of your group.

God's Word calls us to respond by being drawn into deeper trust of God. This section helps you to apply Scripture to your personal lives and to call you to greater intimacy and vulnerability with God.

APPLICATION QUESTIONS
BEARING WITNESS TO JESUS IN THE WORLD
Strengthened by God's Word, we can encourage and engage with our brothers and sisters in Christ in a more meaningful and productive way. The questions in this section will invite you to apply what you are learning.

WEEK 1

THE LIVING SAVIOR AND HIS CALL TO HIS CHURCH

REVELATION 1–2:17

OPENING PRAYER:

Almighty Father, you have promised that your Son would return to be the King of kings and Lord of lords. We wait with holy anticipation. Thank you that Jesus is with us now, guiding his churches and his people. Give us eyes to see and ears to hear what you have for each of us to glean from these ancient words of Revelation. We desire to be blessed as we learn more about Jesus. Unveil our eyes to see the majesty and glory of Jesus. Relate these words to our everyday lives so that we may be men and women who follow the Lamb of God, Jesus. Amen.

KEY VERSE:

> "But he laid his right hand on me, saying, 'Fear not, I am the first and the last, and the living one. I died, and behold I am alive forevermore, and I have the keys of Death and Hades'". (Revelation 1:17b–18)

INTRODUCTION:

In the book of Revelation, we will see a new dimension of Jesus Christ—his glory, majesty, and power. He appears to John, the apostle, in his glory. But he has a message that he wants John to record. This message is for his beloved churches. Seven different churches are addressed that were existing churches at that time in history. Each church had some good things going for it, but there were also problems that needed addressing. These messages ring true to the church today. If we are open, we can see aspects of each church in our lives and possibly in our church. The good news is that Jesus does not give up on these churches or on us. His desire is that we be all he has called us to be.

OPENING QUESTIONS:

1. What are your thoughts as you begin the study of Revelation?

2. This book is about the revealing or unveiling of Jesus Christ. What are your impressions of Jesus at this point in your faith walk?

3. The Gospels reveal certain characteristics about Jesus. Which ones appeal to you?

VIDEO:

The Living Savior and His Call to His Church

VIDEO NOTES:

Jesus appears in glory. He is not the gentle Shepherd or the Suffering Servant. He has taken off his robes of humanity, and his deity is shining forth. His message to the first church in Ephesus is that they have forsaken their first love. They were doing some things quite well, but their love and passion for the person of Jesus has grown cold. His love for them will not let them stay in that place.

Smyrna is the second church, and they are suffering persecution but are remaining steadfast. To the world, they looked poor and afflicted, but in the eyes of Jesus they are rich. They are poor in worldly things but rich in spirit. They are up against Satan's followers (the *"synagogue of Satan,"* 2:9) but Jesus encourages them to not be afraid. Their faithfulness even to the point of death will result in the crown of life which lasts for an eternity.

Pergamum is doing moderately well and has withstood persecution. They are in the nucleus of evil because Satan lives there, as Jesus put it (2:13). False teachings and compromise have infiltrated their ranks. Sexual immorality and the idolatry that can accompany it were making their way into the church. God's grace was being exchanged for immorality and greed. They needed to clean up their church and go back to the basics of Christianity, or Jesus would judge them soon with his double-edged sword.

Read Revelation 1:1–2:17

SCRIPTURE QUESTIONS:

1. What do you think is meant by the description of Jesus as *"the Alpha and the Omega"* (1:8)?

2. Jesus is in the midst of the lampstands which represent the churches, and he is holding the stars which represent the angels of the churches (1:12–13, 20). What does this picture symbolize to you?

APPLICATION QUESTIONS:

1. How do you know if you have "forsaken" your first love, Jesus?

2. Smyrna seems to be in the devil's territory. Have you ever felt that your life is in the pit? How does this message to Smyrna encourage you?

3. Tolerating false teachings, sexual immorality, and deceit (*"the teaching of Balaam,"* 2:14) are strategies that the enemy uses to waylay a church or individual. How can we identify these pitfalls?

CLOSING PRAYER:

Thank you, Lord, that you continually draw us back to you when we fall. Quicken to us areas in our lives we need to address so that we can be faithful followers of Jesus Christ. We desire to be the overcomers. Give us eyes to see and ears to hear your voice. We ask this in Jesus's name. Amen.

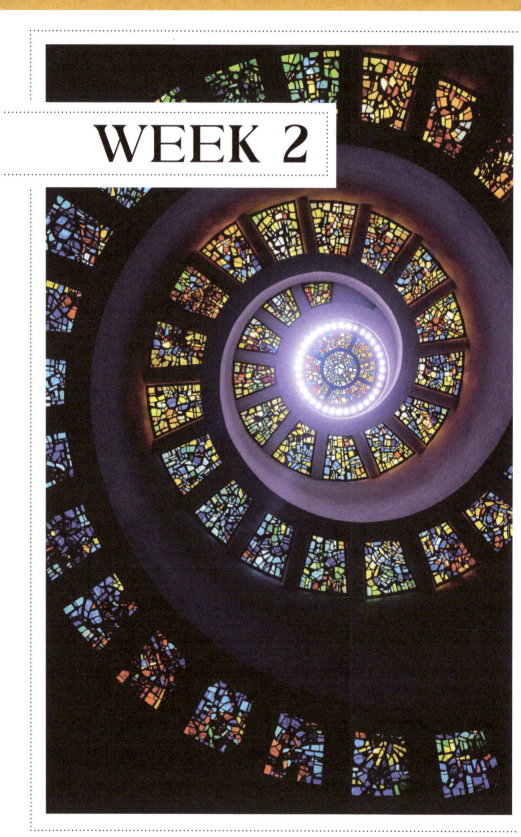

WEEK 2

A SAVIOR WHO DOESN'T GIVE UP

REVELATION 2:18–3:22

OPENING PRAYER:

Holy and merciful Father, it has been your plan all along to involve mankind in building your kingdom on earth as it is in heaven. It is through your church that you will accomplish your task. Thank you that these report cards to the ancient churches still speak to us today. Guide us in applying the warnings and commendations to our faith journey so that we can be all you call us to be. Quicken our church leaders to be on guard against the forces that can compromise the purity of our church. Give us eyes to see and ears to hear. We pray this in the name of the Savior of the church, Jesus Christ. Amen.

KEY VERSE:

> "Those whom I love, I reprove and discipline, so be zealous. Behold, I stand at the door and knock. If anyone hears my voice and opens the door, I will come in to him and eat with him, and he with me." (Revelation 3:19–20)

INTRODUCTION:

Jesus accepts us where we are, but he refuses to leave us there. His report cards to the last of the seven churches of the Revelation exemplify this truth. Jesus reveals truth for the churches, areas in which they are compromised in their faith. This report card series begins with Jesus commending them for what they have done well. Next he reveals the issues that need to be addressed and changed. Finally, he encourages them with the rewards for those who overcome. Notice there seems to be a remnant who always overcome. Jesus doesn't forget them.

OPENING QUESTIONS:

1. As you read through these various churches, which ones do you identify with?

2. Do you think there is a ranking of sinfulness, with one sin being greater than another?

3. Notice that each overcomer is rewarded. What does this say to you about God's justice?

VIDEO:

A Savior Who Doesn't Give Up

VIDEO NOTES:

The last four churches are a mixed bag. Thyatira is doing more than it did at first for the kingdom of God, but there is a major problem, and Jesus will not let it slide. They are tolerating Jezebel, a prophetess who is leading the people into sexual immorality and idolatry. It seems the Lord has tried to reach her, but she is not willing. Jesus seems to be drawing a line in the sand for those who are under her influence to step away or they will experience the same suffering. Notice the purpose of the suffering is for the people to turn to repentance.

Sardis is the next church, and it is dead. The world and the church itself think it is alive. What had they done to receive such condemnation? They were walking in disobedience. They had drifted away from the message of Jesus. The message to this church teaches us to always take stock of where we are in our faith journey and where we are as a church.

The gold star goes to the church in Philadelphia. Amidst persecution from so-called Jews, they have held firm. I love that Jesus knows they were tired and that the trials they had been enduring were difficult. Yet he is their strength. He paints a picture of how they will be redeemed to give them encouragement. They are pillars for all churches to admire and follow.

Laodicea is the church most like churches in our world today. They are wealthy and influential but lukewarm. This is abhorrent to Jesus. He wants all of his people to have a passion for him. He gave his all for the church, and he desires nothing less than our all for him. However, he has not given up on them. He is knocking at the door to their hearts for entry. All they need to do is open the door and Jesus will be with them at the table of communion.

Read Revelation 2:18–3:22.

SCRIPTURE QUESTIONS:

1. Sexual immorality and idolatry seem to pop up again and again in these verses. How do you think it coincides with idolatry?

2. The rewards for these churches are as follows: authority over the nations, the morning star, a permanent name in the book of life, acknowledgment before God, a pillar and permanent place in the temple of God, and the right to sit with Jesus on his throne. What do you think these things mean?

APPLICATION QUESTIONS:

1. Lukewarmness or ho-hum attitudes towards Jesus seem to be abhorrent to him. How do we guard against this attitude?

2. In today's culture, how do we stand firm for the truth of Jesus? How important is Christian community in achieving this?

3. Each of us may have fallen into the clutches of one or more of these pitfalls. What do you notice about each church that turns and repents?

CLOSING PRAYER:

We thank you, Father, that you love us where we are but refuse to leave us there. Like any good father, you are there to discipline, guide, protect and love us to wholeness and fullness of life. We open the doors of our hearts to receive your love and your discipline. Ignite the Holy Spirit in each of us to convict us where we are straying. May we hear your voice affirming our path as we strive to be all you have called us to be. To the glory of you and your Son, Jesus. Amen.

WEEK 3

BEHIND THE VEIL... HEAVEN IS FOR REAL

OPENING PRAYER:

God of all glory and might, we are awed by your majesty. Worthy are you and worthy is the Lamb, Jesus, of all praise and glory. We thank you that Jesus is our Passover Lamb who takes away the sin of the world. He is no longer a helpless Lamb but the mighty being who is worthy to open the scrolls that begin your final judgment. Open our hearts to hear your voice and come to your saving grace. Thank you for always being a Father who pursues your people, that we may have both eternal life and fullness of life on earth. We pray this inJesus's holy name. Amen.

KEY VERSE:

> "And one of the elders said to me, 'Weep no more; behold, the Lion of the tribe of Judah, the Root of David, has conquered, so that he can open the scroll and its seven seals.'" (Revelation 5:5)

INTRODUCTION:

The curtain is pulled back, and God unveils the reality of who Jesus is. We are being shown a heavenly reality that has earthly repercussions. Whether the judgments are symbolic or real seems immaterial. What we do know is that Jesus will be the catalyst of cosmic change and that God loves his people. If God cannot win our hearts through love, at some point in time, he will seek to win our hearts through judgment. As depicted in these chapters, the time of tribulation produces a great harvest of people coming to faith in Jesus as their Savior.

OPENING QUESTIONS:

1. How do you envision heaven? Has your vision of heaven changed over the years?

2. As we read about the power of the slain Lamb, Jesus, what does this reveal about him that you didn't know before?

VIDEO:

Behind the Veil... Heaven Is for Real

VIDEO NOTES:

Chapter 5 is glorious and majestic, but it soon turns dark. Chapter 6 features what has been called the Four Horses of the Apocalypse. This chapter may be an outline as to what is to come or could be the beginning of the birth pangs of the new age. What we know is that things get bad for those living on earth. There will be conquests with conspiracy (the first seal: white horse); absence of peace where man will kill man in unimaginable numbers (the second seal: red horse); worldwide famine but only for the poor (the third seal: black horse); death and destruction of masses of people (the fourth seal: pale horse). Then there is a reprieve. We see martyrs in the fifth seal who are calling to God for justice, followed by unthinkable physical earthly and heavenly disturbances (the sixth seal).

God is showing his power in hopes of drawing rebellious people to himself. Does it work? Chapter 7 makes it clear that God is in control of all these happenings. Some people will refuse him and curse him, but the Jewish people seem to have an about-face. There are 144,000 from the twelve tribes of Israel that have a special calling.

BEFORE CLASS

Read Revelation 4:1–7:17.

SCRIPTURE QUESTIONS:

1. Why do you think Scripture refers to the Lamb as the Lion of Judah and the Root of David?

2. Compare Revelation 6:10 to Romans 12:17–21.

3. Revelation 7:15–17 is similar to Old Testament verses in Isaiah 4 and 49. What does this tell you about the character of God the Father?

APPLICATION QUESTIONS:

1. It seems in Revelation 5:8 that those closest to God's throne are holding "golden bowls of incense, which are the prayers of the saints." What do you think these prayers may be?

2. There is martyrdom during this time. Has there been a time in your life when you were abused, unfairly treated, or rejected and you wanted God to set things right?

3. How do these verses encourage you?

CLOSING PRAYER:

Father, you are a just God and you know the hearts and minds of all people. Help us to wait on you to fulfill your promises.

> "Remember my affliction and my wanderings, the wormwood and the gall. My soul continually remembers it and is bowed down within me. But this I call to mind, and therefore I have hope: the steadfast love of the Lord never ceases; his mercies never come to an end; they are new every morning; great is your faithfulness. "The Lord is my portion," says my soul, "therefore I will hope in him." The Lord is good to those who wait for him, to the soul who seeks him. It is good that one should wait quietly for the salvation of the Lord." (Lamentations 3:19–26)

Thank you, Father, for your faithfulness. We lift up these words in Jesus's name. Amen

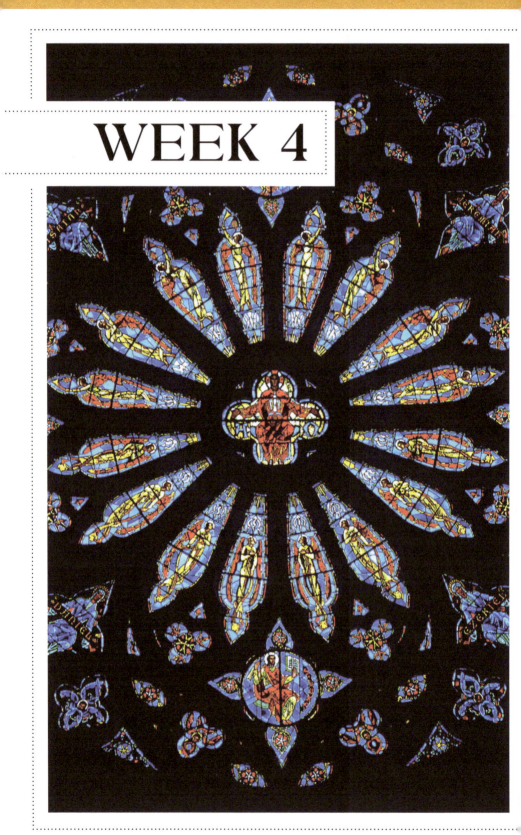

WEEK 4

WHO CAN STAND UNDER GOD'S JUDGMENTS?

OPENING PRAYER:

Holy Father, your love for your creation is evident from the glory of the mountains to the intricacies of insects. Mankind is the crown of your creation and your love for man has never wavered. Give us hearts to receive your love and the tenderness to persevere in that love, even during difficult times. You are a God of love but also a God of judgment. Keep our eyes focused on you through good times and bad, trusting in your love. We pray this in the name that is above every name, Jesus. Amen.

KEY VERSE:

"For the for the accuser of our brothers[a] has been thrown down, who accuses them day and night before our God. 11 And they have conquered him by the blood of the Lamb and by the word of their testimony, for they loved not their lives even unto death." (Revelation 12:10b–11)

INTRODUCTION:

How important are our prayers? It seems that God will silence the adoration of the heavenly hosts to hear the prayers of his people. Our prayers matter. Slowly, the judgments are getting more and more intense. John is told to eat a little scroll—a scroll which is not to be confused with the scroll that was opened by the Lamb. This one tasted sweet but soured soon in his stomach. Symbolizing the future kingdom of God sounds wonderful, but it will involve tragic and difficult choices involving God's judgment. A woman is introduced in chapter 12 who is an explanation of how the battle for man's souls began. The sides are aligned, and the players are moving. Who can survive? Who can stand under these judgments? The answer is found in our memory verse for the week.

OPENING QUESTIONS:

1. Satan was an archangel who desired to take the throne of God. He and his followers lost the battle described in chapter 12. What does this tell you about the power he still has today?

2. The Antichrist represented by the beast and his false prophet have power. It is said there is an Antichrist in each generation. Have you seen this played out in history?

VIDEO:

Who Can Stand Under God's Judgments?

VIDEO NOTES:

Prayers are powerful. They can change the course of history. Prayers can change our lives and the lives of everyone we hold up to the throne of God. During the end times, God will be moving with miracles while Satan is also working his evil ways. The two witnesses of chapter 11 have similarities to the powers of Elijah and Moses. They prophesy, but then are killed, and the people rejoice. Satan has a grip on the people, but the judgments become more intense, and God's kingdom on earth is about to be birthed. On one side you have the beast and the false prophet. On the other side are the two prophets. How do we recognize the good guys and the bad guys? Remember, Satan can masquerade as an angel of light. The answer is the blood of Jesus.

BEFORE CLASS

Read Revelation 8:1–13:18.

SCRIPTURE QUESTIONS:

1. Read Revelation 11:15–18. What does it tell you about the judgments of God and the return of Jesus?

2. Read Revelation 11:19. What is seen? This ancient item was where God met his people. The blood of the sacrifices was poured on its cover which was the atonement cover or mercy seat. Notice that the cover is off. What do you think that symbolizes?

APPLICATION QUESTIONS:

1. Discuss your prayer life. Are we as committed to prayer as we need to be to fight the forces of evil?

2. Revelation 12:10–11 teaches us that we overcome the accuser of the brothers (Satan) by the blood of the Lamb and the word of our testimony. What is your testimony?

CLOSING PRAYER:

Loving Father, you call each of us to battle for your kingdom as prayer warriors. Give us courage to proclaim you to those we encounter. Give us hearts of love for those who are lost. May we be ready at any moment to plead the blood of Jesus over the words of our testimony. Make us ready to speak when you call on us. Help us to speak the truth of you word in love. We pray this in the name of our Savior, Jesus. Amen.

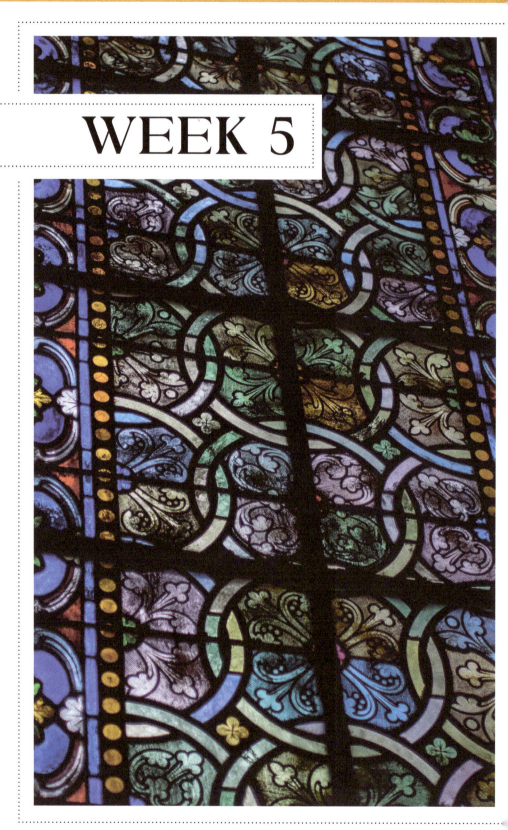

WEEK 5

A BATTLE FOR SOULS, A CHOICE TO BE MADE

REVELATION 14–19:10

OPENING PRAYER:

Faithful Father, you are in the business of transformation. You transformed nothingness into creation. And at the appointed time, you will rid the world of the evil that threatens to destroy it. You will transform our broken world into an eternal, glorious home. Give us minds of wisdom as we go through our lives to be a witness for you and trust in your mighty power. We pray this in the name of the Lamb of God, Jesus. Amen.

KEY VERSE:

> "They will wage war against the Lamb, but the Lamb will triumph over them because he is Lord of lords and King of kings—and with him will be his called, chosen and faithful followers." (Revelation 17:14)

INTRODUCTION:

Since the Garden of Eden, a battle has waged for the souls of mankind. God has sought to woo mankind back to his love. But the choice was theirs. Over the centuries, the enemy, Satan, used deceit and lies to draw man away from the loving grace of God. At some point in time, God will move to rid the earth of the evil that controls it. The battle is real today. The choice is ours today. What is your choice?

OPENING QUESTIONS:

1. How do you see a battle for souls being played out in our world today?

2. How do you make choices for good? What is helpful for you in choosing God's ways? What is most challenging for you in choosing good and not evil?

VIDEO:

A Battle for Souls, a Choice to Be Made

VIDEO NOTES:

The battle for the souls of man is an ongoing one, century to century, year to year, day to day. Idolatry will be rampant in the end times. The abomination that causes desolation will be in full force as people are forced to bear the mark of the beast which allows them to buy and sell. This mark signifies the worship of the Antichrist. This is the line drawn in the sand. From the beginning, God made it clear that we were to worship only him. How do we combat the wiles of Satan and the Antichrist? Revelation 14:12 states, *"Here is a call for the endurance of the saints, those who keep the commandments of God and their faith in Jesus."* At some point God will say "It is done!" His plan for a new creation, a new people is done. The time is up.

BEFORE CLASS

Read Revelation 14:1–19:10.

SCRIPTURE QUESTIONS:

1. What are the comparisons between the woman in chapter 12 and the woman in chapter 15?

2. Despite the horrific judgments, we read in 16:9, 16:11, and 16:21 that the people refused to repent and turn to God. What does this tell you about the importance of repentance?

3.   Reading chapter 18, what are the characteristics of Babylon the Great?

4.   If Babylon represents wealth and privilege, how do we "*come out of her*" (18:4)?

APPLICATION QUESTIONS:

1.   What keeps us from choosing Jesus today?

2.   How have you felt the battle of good and evil in your life?

3.   The wedding supper of the Lamb is glorious. Jesus referred to this banquet several times in the Gospels. We are all invited. Have you sent in your reply card? Compare the wedding of the Lamb to the atrocities of Babylon.

CLOSING PRAYER:

Faithful Father, your desire is that all would come to faith in you and your Son, Jesus Christ. Thank you that you send your Holy Spirit to teach us and guide us. We know that it is only through your Spirit that we will patiently endure through the end times. Strengthen us daily for the ongoing battles in our lives and give us the wisdom to identify when the enemy is deceiving us with lies. May we always know and believe the truth of Jesus. We ask this in the name of our King and Lord, Jesus. Amen.

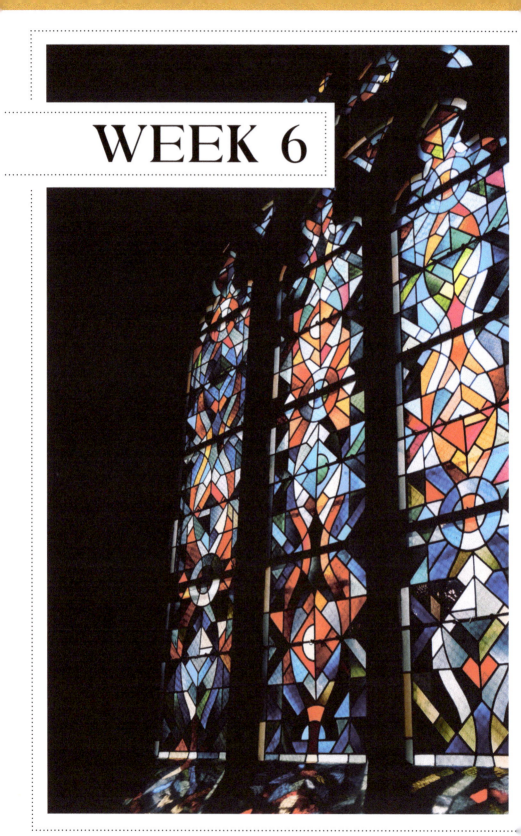

WEEK 6

HE IS COMING! A PROMISE FULFILLED

REVELATION 19:11–22

OPENING PRAYER:

Glorious Father, maker of heaven and earth, Father of our Lord Jesus Christ, we stand in awe of you. We praise your holy name for the sacrifice of your beloved Son, Jesus. It is by his blood that we are healed. It is by his love that we are saved. It is by his resurrection that we are promised eternal life. Your plan for each one of us is more than we can comprehend. Give us courage to walk in the path of obedience so that your kingdom will come on earth as it is in heaven. Give us opportunities to produce eternal fruit by proclaiming your name to those who do not know you. Give us eyes to see and ears to hear your Holy Spirit's promptings. We love you and honor you as the only true God. Thank you that through your Son we can approach you as our "abba" daddy, a father of love and compassion. We give all glory to you and your Son, Jesus Christ, the Savior of the world. Amen.

KEY VERSE:

"The Spirit and the Bride say, "Come." And let the one who hears say, "Come." And let the one who is thirsty come; let the one who desires take the water of life without price." (Revelation 22:17)

INTRODUCTION:

History is going somewhere. Our lives are going somewhere. God's justice will prevail. Those who claim Jesus need not worry about the wrath of God because they are washed clean by the blood of Jesus, the slain Lamb. Those who do not claim Jesus will be judged and will fall short. Our lives on earth are only the beginning, the preface, of the larger story of our eternal lives.

It will be in the new heaven and the new earth that our lives will truly begin, and it will be glorious. This has been God's plan from the beginning, and now at the end of Revelation he announces, "It is done!"

OPENING QUESTIONS:

1. What has been your biggest takeaway from the study of the book of Revelation?

2. Has this study given you peace about the issues that threaten our world today?

3. What does the sovereignty of God mean to you and your life?

VIDEO:

He Is Coming! A Promise Fulfilled

VIDEO NOTES:

God's plan is done! Jesus, the slain Lamb, is victorious. Jesus, the warrior, breaks through time and defeats the forces of evil. Judgment is pronounced, and that judgment is fair. God's people are rewarded while those who refuse God and Jesus are allowed their choice. Our eternal home appears from heaven, and it is glorious. God's light diffuses any darkness, and Jesus is the lamp through which his light is projected. Does this all sound too good to be true? That is the whole point of Revelation. To let you know that it is true. God will triumph. Evil will be destroyed, and God will live with his people forever.

Read Revelation 19:11–22:21.

SCRIPTURE QUESTIONS:

1. The battle for the souls of men has been raging since the fall in the Garden of Eden. What does chapter 19:10–21 say about the final battle at Armageddon?

2. The great white throne of judgment is described in chapter 20:11–15. What do you see as the outcome?

APPLICATION QUESTIONS:

1. Chapter 21 is a glorious chapter with a description of the eternal home. How do these words encourage you? What captures your imagination the most?

2. In chapter 22:1–6, there is a tree whose leaves are for the healing of the nations. There is a history of nations (tribes or peoples) fighting against each other since the beginning of recorded time. What do you think the tree's healing involves?

3. Several times in the last chapter, Jesus says, *"I am coming soon."* However, it is now over two thousand years later, and Jesus has not returned. If this can also mean Jesus returning to usher you "home" at death, how does this make you feel? See also John 14:1–3.

CLOSING PRAYER:

Almighty Father, all glory, laud and honor to you and your Son, Jesus. We eagerly await the time when we will see your face and be in your presence eternally. We stand ready as the Bride of Christ to invite all to "come"—to come to the saving grace you offer through your Son, Jesus Christ. We praise you for the streams of living water Jesus offered to those who follow him. We praise you that the water is available to any who come. You are the Father of abounding love, mercy, and grace, and we adore and worship you. We commit our lives, our hearts, and our strength to you as fellow workmen for your kingdom. In our Savior's name we pray. Amen.

APPENDICES

FREQUENTLY ASKED QUESTIONS

WHAT DO WE DO ON THE FIRST NIGHT OF OUR GROUP?

Have a party! A "get to know you" coffee, dinner, or dessert is a great way to launch a new study. You may want to review the Small Group Covenant (page 149) and share the names of a few friends you can invite to join you. But most importantly, have fun before your study time begins.

WHERE DO WE FIND NEW MEMBERS FOR OUR GROUP?

Finding members can be difficult/challenging, especially for new groups that have only a few people or for existing groups that have lost a few people along the way. We encourage you to pray with your group and then brainstorm a list of people from work, church, your neighborhood, your children's school, family, the gym, and so forth. Use the five circles on page 148 to identify potential group members with whom you would like to build a spiritual friendship. Have each group member invite several people on his or her list.

No matter how you find members, it is vital that you stay on the lookout for new people to join your group. All groups tend to go through healthy attrition—the result of moves, sending out new leaders, ministry opportunities, and so forth—and if the group gets too small, it could be at risk of ending. If you and your group stay open to ideas, you will be amazed at the people God sends your way. The next person just might become a friend for life.

HOW LONG WILL THIS GROUP MEET?

Most groups meet weekly for at least their first six weeks, but every other week can work as well. We strongly recommend that the group meet for the first six months on a weekly basis if possible. This allows for continuity and, if people miss a meeting, they aren't gone for a whole month.

At the end of this study, group members may decide if they want to continue for another study. Some groups launch relationships for years to come, and others are steppingstones into another group experience. Either way, enjoy the journey.

CAN WE DO THIS STUDY ON OUR OWN?

Absolutely! One of the best ways to do this study is not with a full house but with a few friends. You may choose to gather with another couple who would enjoy some relational time (perhaps going to the movies or having a quiet dinner) and then walking through this six-week study. Jesus will be with you even if there are only two of you (Matthew 18:20).

WHAT IF THIS GROUP IS NOT WORKING FOR US?

Group changes are normal. They could be the result of a personality conflict, life stage difference, geographical distance, level of spiritual maturity, or any number of things. Relax. Pray for God's direction, and at the end of this six-week study, decide whether to continue with this group or find another. You don't typically buy the first car you test drive or marry the first person you date, and the same goes with a group. However, don't give up before the six weeks are up—God might have something to teach you. Also, don't run from conflict or judge people before you have given them a chance. God is still working in your life, too!

WHO IS THE LEADER?

Most groups have an official leader. But ideally, the group will mature, and members will rotate the leadership of meetings. We have discovered that healthy groups rotate leaders and homes on a regular basis. This model ensures that all members grow, make their unique contributions, and develop their gifts. This study guide and the Holy Spirit can keep things on track even when you rotate leaders. Christ has promised to be in your midst as you gather. Ultimately, God is your leader each step of the way.

HOW DO WE HANDLE THE CHILDCARE NEEDS IN OUR GROUP?

Child care can be a sensitive issue. We suggest that you empower the group to openly brainstorm solutions. You may try one option that works for a while and then adjust over time. Our favorite approach is for adults to meet in one room and share the cost of a babysitter (or two) who can watch the children in a different part of the house. This way, parents don't have to be away from their children all evening when their children are too young to be left at home. A second option is to use one home for the children and a second home (close by or a phone call away) for the adults. A third idea is to rotate the responsibility of providing a lesson or care for the children either in the same home or in another home nearby. This can be an incredible blessing for young families. Finally, the most common solution is to decide that you need to have a night to invest in your spiritual lives individually or as a couple and to make your own arrangements for childcare. No matter what decision the group makes, the best approach is to dialogue openly about both the need and the solution.

CIRCLES
OF
LIFE

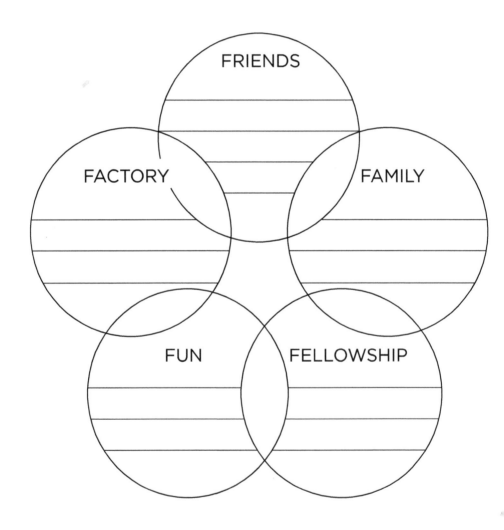

SMALL GROUP COVENANT

OUR PURPOSE
To provide a predictable environment where participants experience authentic Christian community to grow spiritually.

GROUP ATTENDANCE
To give priority to the group meeting. We will call or email if we will be late or absent. (Completing the Group Calendar on p. 150 will minimize this issue.)

SAFE ENVIRONMENT
To help create a safe place where people can be heard and feel loved. (Please, no quick answers, snap judgments, or simple fixes.)

RESPECT DIFFERENCES
To be gentle and gracious with different spiritual maturity levels, personal opinions, temperaments, or "imperfections" in fellow group members. We are all works in progress.

CONFIDENTIALITY
To keep anything that is shared strictly confidential and within the group, and to avoid sharing improper information about those outside the group.

ENCOURAGEMENT FOR GROWTH
To be not just takers, but givers of life. We want to spiritually multiply our lives by serving others with our God-given gifts.

SHARED OWNERSHIP
To remember that every member is a minister and to ensure that each attender will share a small team role or responsibility over time.

ROTATING HOSTS, FACILITATORS, AND HOMES
To encourage different people to host the group in their homes and to rotate the responsibility of facilitating each meeting. (See the Group Calendar on p. 150.)

SMALL GROUP CALENDAR

Planning and calendaring can help ensure the greatest participation at every meeting. At the end of each meeting, review this calendar. Be sure to include a regular rotation of host homes and facilitators, and don't forget birthdays, socials, church events, holidays, and ministry projects.

DATE	SESSION	HOST HOME

SNACKS	FACILITATOR

PRAYER &
PRAISE
JOURNAL

1

2

3

4

5

6

SMALL GROUP ROSTER

NAME	EMAIL	CELL PHONE

SMALL GROUP LEADER HELPS

If you're starting a new group, try planning an Open House before your first formal group meeting. Even if you have only a few members, it's a great way to break the ice and prayerfully consider who else might be open to joining you over the next few weeks. You can also use this kick-off meeting to hand out books, spend some time getting to know each other, discuss each person's expectations for the group, and briefly pray for each other. A simple meal or dessert always make a kickoff meeting more fun. After people introduce themselves and share how they ended up being at the meeting (you can play a game to see who has the wildest story!), have everyone respond to a few icebreaker questions, such as:

- What is your favorite family vacation?
- What is one thing you love about your church?
- What is one thing about your life growing up that most people here don't know?

Next, ask everyone to tell what he or she hopes to get out of the study. You might want to review the Small Group Covenant on p. 149 and talk about each person's expectations and priorities. Finally, set an open chair (maybe two) in the center of your group and explain that it represents someone who would enjoy or benefit from this group who isn't here yet.

Ask people to pray about inviting someone to join the group over the next few weeks. Hand out postcards and have everyone write an invitation or two. Don't worry about ending up with too many people; you can always have one discussion circle in the living room and another in the dining room after you watch the lesson. Each group could then report prayer requests and progress at the end of the session.

You can skip this kickoff meeting if your time is limited, but you'll experience a huge benefit if you take the time to connect with one another in this way.

LEADING FOR THE FIRST TIME

Sweaty palms are a healthy sign. The Bible says that God is gracious to the humble. Remember who is in control; the time to worry is when you're not worried. God will work through those who are soft in heart (and sweaty-palmed).

Seek support. Ask your leader, co-leader, or a close friend to pray for you and prepare with you before the session. Walking through the study will help you anticipate potentially difficult questions and discussion topics.

Bring your uniqueness to the study. Lean into who you are and how God wants you to lead the study.

Prepare. Prepare. Prepare. Go through the session and read the section of Scripture. If you are using the video, listen to the teaching segment. Consider writing in a journal or praying through the day to prepare yourself for what God wants to do. Don't wait until the last minute to prepare.

Ask for feedback so you can grow. Perhaps in an email or on index cards handed out at the study, have everyone write down three things you did well and one thing you could improve on. Don't get defensive. Instead, show an openness to learn and grow.

Share with your group what God is doing in your heart. God is searching for those whose hearts are fully his. Share your trials and victories, people will relate.

Prayerfully consider whom you would like to pass the baton to next week. God is ready for the next member of your group to go on the faith journey you just traveled. Make it fun and expect God to do the rest.

LEADERSHIP TRAINING 101

Congratulations! You have responded to the call to help shepherd Jesus's flock. There are few other tasks in the family of God that surpass the contribution you will be making. As you prepare to lead, here are a few thoughts to keep in mind. We encourage you to read these and review them with each new discussion leader.

1. Remember that you are not alone. God knows everything about you, and he knew that you would be asked to lead this group. Remember that it is common for all good leaders to feel that they are not ready to lead. Moses, Solomon, Jeremiah, and Timothy were all reluctant to lead. God promises, *"I will never leave you nor forsake you"* (Hebrews 13:5). Whether you are leading for one evening, for several weeks, or for a lifetime, you will be blessed as you serve.

2. Don't try to do it alone. Pray right now for God to help you build a healthy leadership team. If you can enlist a co-leader to help you lead the group, you will find your experience to be much richer. This is your chance to involve as many people as you can in building a healthy group. All you have to do is call and ask people to help. You'll probably be surprised at the response.

3. Just be yourself. If you won't be you, who will? God wants you to use your unique gifts and temperament. Don't try to do things exactly like another leader; do them in a way that fits you! Just admit when you don't have an answer and apologize when you make a mistake. Your group will love you for it, and you'll sleep better at night!

4. Prepare for your meeting ahead of time. Review the session and write down your responses to each question. Pay special attention to exercises that ask group members to do something other than engage in discussion, like take an action. These exercises will help your group live what the Bible teaches, not just talk about it.

5. Pray for your group members by name. Before you begin your session, go around the room in your mind and pray for each member. Ask God to use your time together to touch the heart of every person uniquely. Expect God to lead you to whomever he wants you to encourage or challenge in a special way. If you listen, God will surely lead!

6.   When you ask a question, be patient. Someone will eventually respond. Sometimes people need a moment or two of silence to think about the question. Keep in mind, if silence doesn't bother you, it won't bother anyone else. After someone responds, affirm the response with a simple "thanks" or "good job." Then ask, "How about somebody else?" or "Would someone who hasn't shared like to add anything?" Be sensitive to new people or members who aren't ready to share. If you give them a safe setting, they will blossom over time.

7.   Provide transitions between questions. When guiding the discussion, always read aloud the transitional paragraphs and the questions. Ask the group if anyone would like to read the paragraphs or Bible passages. Don't call on anyone, but ask for volunteers; then be patient until someone begins. Be sure to thank the people who read aloud.

8.   Break up into small groups each week or a larger group won't stay. If your group has a lot of people, we strongly encourage you to have the group gather sometimes in discussion circles of three or four people during the **Encounter the Word, Engage Our Hearts, and Encourage Others** sections of the study. With a greater opportunity to talk in small circles, people will connect more with the study, apply more quickly what they're learning, and ultimately get more out of it. A small circle also encourages a quiet person to participate and minimizes the effect of a more dominant or vocal member. It can also help people feel more loved in your group.

     When you gather again at the end of the section, you can have one person summarize the highlights from each circle. Small circles are also helpful during prayer time. People who are not accustomed to praying aloud will feel more comfortable trying it with just two or three others.

     Also, prayer requests won't take as much time, so circles will have more time to actually pray. When you gather back with the whole group, you can have one person from each circle briefly update everyone on the prayer requests. People are more willing to break into small circles to pray if they know the whole group will hear all the prayer requests.

9.   Rotate facilitators weekly. At the end of each meeting, ask the group who should lead the following week. Let the group help select your weekly facilitator. You may be perfectly capable of leading each time, but you will help others grow in their faith and gifts if you give them opportunities to lead. You can use the Small Group Calendar (p. 150) to fill in the names of the different leaders for all the meetings if you prefer.

10. One final challenge (for new or first-time leaders): Before your first opportunity to lead, look up each of the five passages listed below. Read each one as a devotional exercise to help equip yourself with a shepherd's heart. Trust us on this one. If you do this, you will be more than ready to lead your first meeting.

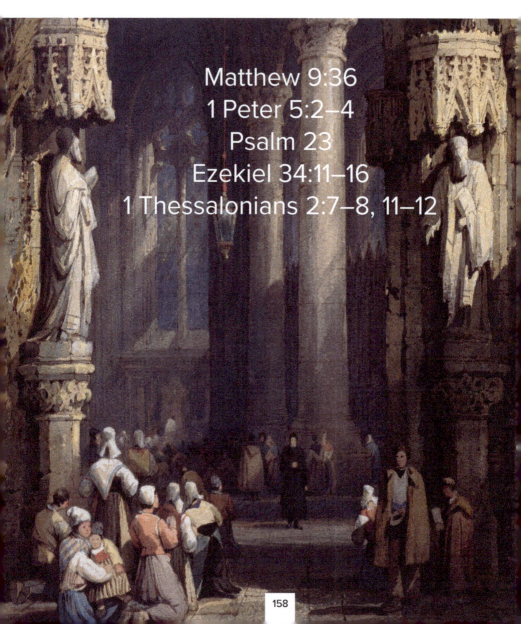

Matthew 9:36
1 Peter 5:2–4
Psalm 23
Ezekiel 34:11–16
1 Thessalonians 2:7–8, 11–12